To the Montair Elementary School Community

Enjoy your journey

Stan Klein

Reflections

from a

Different Journey

❧

What Adults with Disabilities

Wish All Parents Knew

Edited by Stanley D. Klein, Ph.D., and John D. Kemp

Foreword by Marlee Matlin

McGraw·Hill

New York   Chicago   San Francisco   Lisbon   London   Madrid   Mexico City
Milan   New Delhi   San Juan   Seoul   Singapore   Sydney   Toronto

Library of Congress Cataloging-in-Publication Data

Reflections from a different journey : what adults with disabilities wish all parents knew / edited by Stanley D. Klein and John D. Kemp.
 p.   cm.
 ISBN 0-07-142269-2
 1. Parents of children with disabilities.   2. Children with disabilities.   3. People with disabilities.   I. Klein, Stanley D.   II. Kemp, John D.

HQ759.913.R43   2004
649'.151—dc22   2003016996

This book is dedicated to all parents of children with disabilities, the most important experts.

Jason Kingsley's essay, "What I'd Tell That Doctor," on pp. 13–15 contains an excerpt from the book *Count Us In: Growing Up with Down Syndrome* by Jason Kingsley and Mitchell Levitz, published by Harcourt Brace and Company in 1994. It is reprinted with the permission of Harcourt Brace and Company.

Donna F. Smith's essay, "Solutions from the Heart," on pp. 60–64 originally appeared in the May 2003 issue of the "Braille Forum," a monthly publication of the American Council of the Blind, and is being reprinted here with permission. The "Braille Forum" is available in braille, large print, audiocassette, and computer disk, as well as online at acb.org.

1 2 3 4 5 6 7 8 9 0   AGM/AGM   3 2 1 0 9 8 7 6 5 4

ISBN 0-07-142269-2

Interior design by Monica Baziuk

McGraw-Hill books are available at special quantity discounts to use as premiums and sales promotions, or for use in corporate training programs. For more information, please write to the Director of Special Sales, Professional Publishing, McGraw-Hill, Two Penn Plaza, New York, NY 10121-2298. Or contact your local bookstore.

This book is printed on acid-free paper.

CONTENTS

1 Love Me and Accept Me as I Am

2 Parents Are the Most Important Experts

3 Parental Expectations

4 Sexuality

5 Education About Disability

FOREWORD

WHEN JOHN KEMP asked me to write this foreword, I remembered back to when John and I first met in the 1980s in Chicago. I was attending a performance of *Staring Back*, a play dealing with disabilities issues, after having just completed my first film, *Children of a Lesser God*, and John was a young executive with the National Easter Seal Society. We have been friends ever since. In more recent years, I served on the VSA Arts Board while John was serving as the chief executive officer at VSA Arts, an international organization founded by Jean Kennedy Smith in 1974 that creates learning opportunities through the arts for people with disabilities.

When John told me about the plans for *Reflections from a Different Journey*, it sounded interesting. But I was uncertain about it because I was concerned that many people might write to complain about the misdeeds of their parents. This probably occurred to me because now that I am a parent of three children, I sometimes wonder how my kids will remember my efforts. Once I had read a few of the essays, my uncertainty was replaced by excitement, admiration, and pride. When I read John's essay ("Disability Culture") about how his dad demonstrated the importance of public service with his own commitment to service to others, I gained a new appreciation of how John became the wonderful national leader that he continues to be.

In this book, people with all kinds of disabilities make clear that they can be capable role models for children; advisors to their parents and family members; and teachers to educators, health care professionals, and the many other adults who provide services for children with disabilities and their families. In fact, the essays have important messages for all of us as we strive to make our world a more caring, loving, and peaceful place for all children and families.

This book is a wonderful celebration of diversity. The essay writers have grown up with many different kinds of disabilities in many different places, including some countries outside the United States. They are not people who have "overcome" their disabilities. Rather, they have overcome the prejudices of society that all too often stereotype people with disabilities in destructive ways.

As some essay authors describe, they could also have become victimized by another kind of prejudice—the prejudice of prognosis. But, their parents did not accept the predictions of well-intentioned physicians and other professionals. With the love and support of their parents, they were not imprisoned by dire prognoses. Instead, they were encouraged to dream, to try, to make mistakes, to be active participants in the life of their families and communities, and to reject the limitations suggested by scientific and clinical stereotypes. With the help of these essay writers, I hope that "helping professionals" will appreciate that their prognoses may be based on "truths" that have taken years to evolve, may be based on prejudicial attitudes, and may no longer be accurate.

As a person with a disability, I have not overcome my deafness. Nor have I tried to pass as a person without a disability. I am often considered a role model for children growing up with disabilities or called a "representative" of people with disabilities. In these roles, I do my best to remind the world that there are many, many fine people with disabilities who are wonderful role models. These other role models don't happen to enjoy the fame that I do because I won an Academy Award when I was only twenty-one years old and have continued to be a working actress in Hollywood—despite dire predictions that I would never work in Hollywood again and that I only won an Academy Award out of pity. I am an actress who happens to be deaf. Like the essay authors in this book, I have encountered many barriers along the way. At times, I believed what some people said—that I would never be a success in the acting field because I am deaf.

But, as a child with a disability, I was fortunate to grow up in a wonderful, supportive, and loving family. My family encouraged me to not let my disability stand in my way. Although I sometimes experienced frustration related to being deaf, thanks to my family, I felt secure and enabled. With family and community support, I realized that my own attitude about myself was critical to my success. I could make my own successes happen and my dreams come true.

Each essay in this book offers a great deal because the authors have given of themselves to benefit all of us. But I am not going to describe how I reacted to any specific essays, because I want each parent-reader to experience each one—and then share personally meaningful essays with grandparents, other family members, and friends. However, I do want to single out those essays dealing with intimacy and sexuality because they remind us that all human beings need physical and emotional intimacy, love, and respect.

Besides my friend John Kemp, my life has previously been touched by two of the essay authors. In 1994, along with former Miss America Heather Whitestone, I presented an Equality, Dignity, and Independence Award from the National Easter Seal Society to Jason Kingsley and his coauthor, Mitchell Levitz, for their fine book, *Count Us In: Growing Up with Down Syndrome* (Harcourt Brace and Company, 1994). In 1996, my biography was included in *Extraordinary People with Disabilities* (Children's Press, 1996), written by Deborah Kent and Kathryn A. Quinlan. Having recently written a novel called *Deaf Child Crossing* (Simon & Schuster, 2002), I appreciate that writing is hard work.

In Deborah and Kathryn's book, they describe how people with disabilities were considered "useless burdens on society" for thousands of years. In that context, anything a person with a disability managed to accomplish was perceived as amazing. They then write that the title of their book is ironic because, in recent years, people with disabilities have worked very hard to be perceived as regular, ordinary people. Similarly, in the introduction to *Reflections from a Different Journey*, the editors describe the essayists as "relatively ordinary, accomplished individuals"—not superstars. From my own experience, I know that there are many more people with disabilities who have a great deal to offer all of us who are parents and who want our children to learn from the wonderful diversity of our world.

There continue to be unnecessary gaps between people with disabilities and those without disabilities. I am confident that this book will encourage people to get to know some people with disabilities and to find out that we are just like other people—human beings doing our best. If anyone still wonders about the roles that people with disabilities can play in making our world a better place for all people to thrive, this book will convince such skeptics that we are ready, willing, and able. Finally, I hope that readers with disabilities will share the "disability pride" I feel because of the caring and sharing by the essay authors.

In the end, I am reminded of the words of the biblical prophet Micah when he said, "What does the Lord require of you but to do justice, and love kindness, and to walk humbly with your God?" In the context of this book, I hope we will all come to understand that there is room on our earth for all of us, regardless of our perceived abilities.

Marlee Matlin
Los Angeles, California

ACKNOWLEDGMENTS

WE ARE GRATEFUL to all the individuals with disabilities who took the time to write and submit essays for this book as well as to those who assisted some of the essay authors. We are especially grateful to all those who assisted us by spreading the word via the Internet about this book and the organizations that published our request for essays.

We appreciate the suggestions and patience of Sheree Bykofsky and Janet Rosen, our literary agents, and Judith McCarthy, our editor at McGraw-Hill.

We are also thankful for the support and assistance of Meredith Ellis, Sameta Kemp, Sarah Klein, Lauren Smith, and Robert Naseef.

Finally, we appreciate Marlee Matlin's willingness to write the foreword.

INTRODUCTION

PARENTING IS A VITAL and difficult task under any circumstances. While parents of children with disabilities and special health care needs confront the same challenges as other parents, many of the challenges can be more complicated due to a child's unique needs and because, until recently, the world has not welcomed children with disabilities. When parents of children with disabilities wonder about their child's future, they do so with considerable uncertainty since communities—even though they are now more welcoming— often lack personal experience with adults with disabilities.

Communities are becoming increasingly welcoming because of more than fifty years of combined advocacy efforts by parents of children with disabilities and individuals with disabilities. During that time, these advocates have insisted that every human being is entitled to be an active participant not just in a loving family but also in a community and in a world that respect the diversity of the human experience.

Today, in the twenty-first century, young parents of children with disabilities can anticipate that their children will enjoy more and more opportunities to thrive because of the pioneering advocacy efforts by parents and people with disabilities in the twentieth century. Today, the laws of the United States and other countries, as well as the policies of the United Nations, specify that there will be programs that support parents of children with disabilities, the children themselves, and their families. Although existing programs are not always adequate and need continuous improvement, families no longer face the prospect of raising a child with a disability in isolation and against the wishes of the community. As many of the contributors to this book who grew up in the 1950s and 1960s attest, their parents were advised to place their babies or young children in institutions, away from family and community—and forget about them.

Fortunately, few parents "forget" their children. Parents everywhere, including parents who lacked the resources to oppose the prevailing attitudes of society and did institutionalize their children, joined together and began to speak out on behalf of all children with disabilities. Adults with disabilities—those who had managed to grow up in communities and those who had acquired disabilities as a result of accidents, wars, or health—also began to speak out and demand to be included in the life of their communities as equals. In the United States, the voices of parents and people with disabilities began to be heard in a society that had also begun to listen to the voices of diverse groups seeking civil rights and equal opportunities for themselves.

The difficult job of parenting—even when it takes place in welcoming families and communities with long traditions of caring for children and families—is less difficult when parents can turn to experienced parents, family members, and friends for encouragement, support, and advice. For parents of children with disabilities and special health care needs, connecting with experienced parents of children with disabilities has been, and will continue to be, an essential source of comfort, nourishment, information, and advice.

Knowing that experienced, "veteran" parents of a child with a disability and/or special health care needs are the most important sources of emotional support and wisdom for new parents, one of us (SDK) coedited (with Kim Schive) a book of essays by "veteran" parents—*You Will Dream New Dreams: Inspiring Personal Stories by Parents of Children with Disabilities* (Kensington Books, 2001). However, since most of the essays were by veteran parents of children who were still young, the book did not address parental concerns about their child's future as an adult.

The best way for parents to help their children plan for the future is to meet and talk with adults who grew up with disabilities. Having lived the disability experience, such adults are a wonderful source of wisdom and inspiration. Yet, many parents do not have such opportunities. Parents and the health care and education professionals who serve children and their families have begun to appreciate that adults with disabilities can be an important source of emotional support and wisdom. But they lack experience with successful adults with disabilities and are unable to address parental concerns about "What will happen when my child grows up?"

For this book, adults with different kinds of disabilities and/or special health care needs have written short essays for parents—as well as for older children with disabilities, family members, and the education and health care professionals who serve them. In the invitation to prepare these essays, the authors were asked to write about something that they wish their own parents had read or been told while they were growing up. We hope that the range of personal perspectives provides not only emotional support and inspiration but also practical child-rearing information. In addition, we are confident that these essays will instill a stronger sense that adults with disabilities can and do make vital contributions and are tremendous role models as well as advisors to families and professionals.

Through our personal networks and the power of the Internet, we extended invitations to adults with disabilities to contribute to this book. Hundreds of adults responded from the United States and many other countries. The caring and wisdom of all the essays exceeded our expectations. So many people were willing to offer so much. We are very appreciative of the efforts of all the writers of all the essays, the friends and family members who assisted some essay authors, and all the people who helped us by spreading the word about our invitation throughout the world.

Although many essays offered valuable insights, we had to select a relatively small number of essays to create this book. We have included the perspectives of people with many different kinds of disabilities. While the messages have much in common, they also offer many specifics, some unique to certain types of disabilities. Despite these variations, the powerful commonality across all the essays—including those that were not selected for the book—is the humanity of people with disabilities. Regardless of the type of disability, the essays illustrate that people with disabilities are, first and foremost, human beings—with the same needs and desires as people without disabilities. At the same time, the essay authors and their families confronted prejudice and many other obstacles that are unique to being a person with a disability.

Our essay writers are relatively ordinary, accomplished individuals—they are not superstars. All too often, the media focuses its attention on the relatively few individuals who happen to have disabilities who do extraordinary things. The result is a different kind of prejudice—people with disabilities are to be superstars. While such an attitude may be an improvement over excluding people with disabilities from participation in community life, we hope that this book will illustrate that people with disabilities are just like everyone else—each with his or her own strengths and limitations, striving for a decent quality of life.

Once we had sorted through all the essays and decided which ones to include, we struggled with how to present them within this book. We decided to organize them by themes—even though as you'll see, some of the essays touch on several different themes. Nonetheless, we believe that the essays can be read in any order, reread, and shared with others—one at time, any time, and in any order.

Before describing the themes, we believe it is essential to note several "editorial" decisions we made. First, all essays have been edited to put "people first." Accordingly, we always speak of our essay writers as people—with a disability. We do not use such terms as the *handicapped*, the *crippled*, the *learning disabled*, or the *mentally ill*. We believe using such terms is demeaning because any person's disability does not define that individual. However, since people with disabilities are unique as are all other individuals, we acknowledge that some fine, respectable people with disabilities do not share our view regarding language.

Our other editorial decision has to do with the specific diagnostic terminology that is used to describe one specific type of disability or another. Many people, including many essay authors, use capital letters in naming their own specific disability. We have edited to fit the scientific style in which capitalization is only used when the diagnostic condition has been named in recognition of the clinician or scientist who first described it in the scientific literature—for example, Down syndrome or Duchenne muscular dystrophy. Other than these two editorial changes, the words in the essays that follow are the writer's own.

"Love and Accept Me as I Am" is the theme of the first group of essays. In these essays, the authors express their appreciation for parents who provided unconditional love and a sense of belonging in a family; for parents who accepted them as whole people—including that part of them considered to be a disability. Some essayists in this section are explicitly critical of things their parents did. But, they make their criticisms with love and care and with minimal resentment.

"Parents Are the Most Important Experts" is the theme of the second group of essays. These authors describe how their parents addressed their unique needs and became the most important experts in the lives of their children.

The third grouping deals with "Parental Expectations"—a complex area for all parents and children. The essayists in this section, while agreeing that having a specific disability or disease may impose some limitations, present different approaches to expectations and standards. They make clear that it is appropriate to ask a child with a disability what she or he wants to be as a grown-up and to encourage every child to have hopes and aspirations.

Because it can be an especially difficult topic for parents and children, "Sexuality" has a separate section even though it is, in part, a topic that deals with expectations. These essays make clear that children with disabilities, just like all other children, need to talk about and learn about intimacy and sexuality—because intimacy and sexuality are important to everyone's identity and because silence on these subjects is a destructive message.

"Education About Disability" is the fifth theme. These essays describe the importance, for both parents and children, of learning about a child's disability and how to facilitate necessary accommodations so that each child can expect to enjoy a full life.

We conclude with an essay on "Disability Culture" because it provides a perspective that is evident throughout many of the essays in the book. We hope it will enable parents to nurture a child's identity as a valued member of society as well as a valued member of a unique culture—disability culture.

At the end of *Reflections from a Different Journey*, we have included a brief resources section that identifies Internet sites where parents may find additional useful support and information. We also encourage all parents to seek out adults with disabilities as well as other parents of children with disabilities. These people have the most priceless information.

1

LOVE ME
AND ACCEPT ME
AS I AM

AIN'T DONE TOO BAD FOR A CAULIFLOWER

Ross Flood

D URING THE EARLY 1950S, *a young New Zealand woman pushed her baby's pram down Auckland City's Queen Street. Her tears of anger indicated that this was no ordinary stroll down the main street of her country's biggest city. She had just come from a doctor's appointment. The doctor had advised her to put her child in an institution and forget about him. She was told her son would be a "vegetable" all his life—with no chance of improvement. Through her veil of tears, she peered into her baby's smiling face and saw the spark of intelligence. Within that moment, she made the decision to take her baby home and prove the medical professional wrong.*

Those tears of anger belonged to my mother. The toothless smile was my own.

I must admit my intelligence has been called into question more than once since that decision was made—especially during my madcap youth. However, overall, this "cauliflower" has had a quality of life far from the prophecy of vegetation.

On that fateful day, my mother took me back to a loving family—my father, sister, and grandmother. Each one endorsed my mother's decision and set about laying the foundation for me to become a full-fledged member of society.

Right from the start, I was plunged into the mainstream. Weekly visits to the local picture theater were to be the norm, and, since we were great followers of our national game of Rugby Union, every wintry Saturday we were at the park cheering on our local heroes. And there were birthdays to celebrate, and Christmas and Easter holidays to look forward to. During the year, I set about earning Boy Scout badges while my sister, Jackie, involved herself with Girls Brigade activities.

My family gave me a sense of belonging and the ability to be confident in a nondisabled world. They gave me the basic skills that I developed to cope with everyday situations. At times they also had the strength to bite their lips, stand back, and allow me to make my own mistakes. My family's acceptance was unconditional. But, at vital stages of my life, society has not supported their decision— especially when it came to career and job opportunities.

My schooling started at a special school for children with cerebral palsy. There the emphasis was on improving my physical condition—quite rightly so. However, because of my physical disabilities, any thoughts of career options were put on the back burner. At the age of twelve, I was declared fit enough to attend mainstream schooling.

Unfortunately, because I lagged far behind my age group academically, I was put into classes with classmates three or four years my junior. Although the kids were very good to me, I have to admit the age gap did affect my performance. I also missed the solidarity of peers with interests more compatible to my own. Often, during my school days, convenient decisions were made that were not always in my best interest. For example, authorities put me in the most accessible class rather than the most academically suitable.

Looking back on this period of my life, I really missed having a mentor with some personal knowledge of disability. The closest person to a mentor that I can remember was a teacher with cerebral palsy at the special school. Being associated with this teacher gave me an inkling of how my life might unfold. Unfortunately, her influence was left behind as I ventured out to my local school. Due to the lack of such support, I drifted in my schoolwork.

Eventually, I left school and was placed in a sheltered workshop. At the workshop, I performed a mind-numbing job of folding cigar box cartons—with the promise of a job dangled in front of me. Instead, after a lengthy period, I was labeled "unemployable"—and shown the door.

Fortunately, I always had my family to fall back on. Each member contributed to my development in a very real way. Except for the time I nearly choked her to death in a play fight on our front lawn, my sister and I have always been great friends. Through her own academic achievement, she always inspired and encouraged me to stretch out and achieve beyond people's expectations of me. My Irish Nana helped fuel my imagination with tales of leprechauns and banshees. My dad encouraged me to put my thoughts on paper by writing reports on rugby games. To my great surprise and delight, my reports were published in the local paper. As a family, we learned to surround ourselves, as much as possible, with people who focused on my capabilities rather than my disabilities.

While we respected the medical specialists' points of view, we always ensured our family made the ultimate decision. A good example of this was the decision concerning surgery on my hands. Due to my cerebral palsy, my hands were permanently twisted, leaving me with very little wrist movement. The surgical procedure involved breaking my wrists and cementing them back together again—with all the tendons and nerves in the right places and in working order. As a result, my wrist would be in a fixed position with my hands straightened out, enabling me to use my hands in a more practical manner. Obviously, this was intricate surgery, with no guarantee of success. The elderly doctor who initially examined me did not fill us with confidence about the benefits of such an operation. So at that time, we, as a family, turned down the opportunity. But some years later, a younger doctor was much more positive about the outcome. This time the surgery took place and was a great success. I had always coped with the way things were. But all of a sudden my hands became much more useful tools.

As a result of these operations, I have been able to do far more for myself. In the years following the surgery, I was even able to drive a car and open up a whole new world for myself. One could argue that I always have had a set of wheels—but, this time, it was different. The wheels were driven by a motor and greatly enhanced my independence. I received far more than a license to drive when I passed my driving examination. It was also a license to explore my opportunities and to challenge earlier decisions that labeled me "of limited use."

I feel that I must leave it to others to comment on whether or not I have proven my worth. But, in my humble opinion, I ain't done too badly for a cauliflower. Listed among my achievements are university graduate, Paralympian, and freelance writer.

There have been some "expert" decisions in my life that have restricted my progress. But everyone of us must accept that we are, to a large degree, a product of our time. I remember Jackie going through a frustrating period during her first job interviews, when the emphasis was placed on the importance of women having a family rather than a career, simply because that was the attitude of the time. My father, a man of obvious intelligence, was pulled out of school at a tender age because he was needed to work in the family grocery shop. They, too, had to battle against constraints that restricted their progress. The optimist within me hopes that we can all shake off negative labels and pursue our dreams unhindered.

Each generation will probably have its problems to solve. Overall, I'm greatly encouraged by the current enlightened attitude toward people with disabilities. I am confident that a more positive attitude combined with advanced technology will lead to better opportunities.

Nevertheless, parents in need of guidance could well consider adopting similar values as those that strongly influenced my upbringing.

The first priority is to give your child a sense of belonging. Second, surround yourself with positive people who emphasize your child's capabilities. Third, when your child suddenly transforms into a young adult have the strength to allow him or her to explore their world with all its exciting possibilities. And, allow them some breathing space, so that they can make their own mistakes. Of course, some sensible parental guidance is required at times. But, believe me, I made my share of mistakes and have lived to tell the tale. If you permit your son or daughter to have as much say in their own development as realistically possible, you will have few regrets.

~

FIFTY-ONE-YEAR-OLD ROSS FLOOD *has cerebral palsy. He is enjoying the experience of entering his sixth decade living in New Zealand's North Island. Ross started writing in his preteen years and has never stopped flirting with the English language. He discovered Auckland University in his late twenties, and, "in between the parties," graduated with a B.A. in Sociology. Since his graduation, he has been employed to write copy for the local airport radio station and as an editor/columnist for several disability publications. Currently, he is producing a publication called* Athletes on Campus *for the Auckland University of Technology.*

Along the way, Ross has discovered an indoor bowls sport called bocce, which has taken him to New York, Argentina, and Portugal, as well as to the 2000 Paralympics in Sydney with the New Zealand team.

Ross's ambition is to continue developing his writing and to make every day an adventure to be experienced to the max.

DISABILITY DOES NOT EQUAL LIABILITY

Pat Danielson

As A PERSON WHO ACQUIRED juvenile rheumatoid arthritis
(JRA) at the age of five, I can attest to the fact it can be very
hard for kids with disabilities to access the information being gained
by their peers. Reasons for this vary from misguided good intentions
to convenience to ignorance.

For example, during a fire drill, I was given permission to stay in
the classroom, "because it's just a drill." Even during everyday activities, negotiating hallways full of pushing, gyrating kids scared the
hell out of me and tested my ability to avoid being trampled. Fire
drills were even worse. I thought that if there were a fire, I'd die
either way, so opting out of drills seemed like a great idea. However,
both school staff and I would have benefited from devising a plan
for my safe exit. But no one spoke of it. I was too young and ignorant to ask; they were too ignorant to offer.

Other times, I was expected to push myself beyond my limits.
The day my third-grade class went for a walking field trip was a tor-
ture test. My entire effort was spent on struggling to walk faster,
while enduring great pain. No matter how hard I pushed myself, I
remained at least one-half block behind my class. If the teacher

talked about the sights, I heard none of it. If the activity was social, it was lost to me. I was entirely alone in my sweating, panting, and aching.

Fortunately, I had parents who believed my illness and resulting disability did not excuse me from family responsibility. I took my turn washing dishes and doing household chores. I was expected to attend school regularly, complete my work to the best of my ability, and hand it in on time. My parents did not tolerate whining and complaining from me any more than from my four siblings. This was very important for my emerging sense of personal responsibility and competence.

Unfortunately, I also learned from my family that my disability, while not a problem at home, was not acceptable in public—as if my JRA were a shameful secret. My parents never actually said that to me, but I believed JRA was not acceptable because it was never mentioned at home. When my parents accommodated me without speaking to me about it, my short life experience told me the reason was because there was something bad about a person who had JRA. It was a "bad" that was personal to me. In the absence of correct information, I attempted to fill in the blanks myself—and did so poorly.

The lack of communication about my disability negated much of the good that came from my family's expectations of me. By acknowledging my disability at home, my parents could have helped me learn to assert my right to exist. I could have learned to identify my needs and ask for help—valuable skills for an adult with a disability.

If the adults in my life had asked whether or not I would be OK with the walking field trip, I could have learned to assess my physical abilities honestly and ascertain the effect that amount of walking might have. I could have learned to tell them it would be fun to go along, but I would never keep up with everyone. The teacher could have altered the length of the walk or offered transportation. With the availability of today's adaptive devices, my parents could have acquired an electric scooter for me. Children shouldn't be left behind because of logistical matters. It's incumbent on the adults and the child who needs help to figure out a way around the problem.

To learn as my peers were learning, I needed to be where they were, doing what they did. If I were unable to do things the same way as my friends, I should have figured out another way rather than believing I had to try to pass as a person with no physical problems. My classmates needed me, and I didn't know how to offer my abilities.

Emphasis is often placed on the disproportionate needs of the one child with a disability and the "sacrifices" made by others on his behalf. I see it differently. Aside from your child's friendship others would miss by not knowing him, consider the rich opportunities presented his classmates to learn to think outside the box merely by associating with your kid. Your child is not, in any way, a liability to the people around him. Friends appreciate and accommodate one another. For everyone's benefit, adults should facilitate and support every child's growing ability to create alternatives.

Your child with a disability needs to learn all the life lessons that kids without disabilities are expected to learn. Additionally, he needs disability-specific information. Parents face the task of balancing the medical, academic, and social/emotional aspects of their child's growth. This task can be challenging when the child's medical needs take him out of school periodically for surgery or physical therapy, or when the child leaves the classroom regularly to work with a therapist or counselor. The child may need several sources of help to make it possible for him to keep up with classmates and succeed. Since the additional help is meant to support the development of your child as an ordinary kid, skillful balance of disability-specific needs with general kid needs is critical.

Achieving this balance means making sure your child is working alongside his or her peers in classrooms, on the playground, and in the community. If the class has group science projects, your child should be an integral part of the group regardless of his or her ability to manipulate test tubes. Physical barriers should not excuse your child from learning—by doing—those concepts.

During recess your child needs to be with peers. If she is unable to jump rope, twirling the rope for others might be her thing. She becomes part of the activity, learning the chants, and even learning the physics of jumping rope with her friends.

If the class volunteers at the homeless shelter, your child needs to be there. If left behind because of physical barriers, he or she will miss sharing the experiences of classmates.

Kids with disabilities must learn to identify their needs and how to communicate them accurately. Cultivating an attitude that asserts "I belong here; I am an important part of life" is also necessary because they are bombarded every day by messages from a society that tells them they are not quite good enough, cost too much to invest in medically and educationally, and, in some instances, should not have been born.

Your child needs to practice putting aside those negative messages while going about the business of learning to be their best self. They have to become an expert on themselves in every way so they will be prepared to question judgments of them.

Disability gives a child great potential for growing to be a resilient, independent, creative person. He or she has to think independently enough not to believe society's devaluation of him or her. They have to be creative enough to figure out how to contribute in a world where much of life takes place up stairs, where vehicles do not accommodate wheelchairs, doorways are not wide enough, and restrooms are too small. They have to figure out how to get hired for a job they are qualified for when the interviewer takes one look at the obvious nature of their disability and decides immediately they aren't worth the trouble.

If parents and significant adults in the lives of kids with disabilities would dream possibilities for that child and teach that child how to pursue dreams, there is little reason to believe the child cannot grow to be a successful adult. It starts with expecting kids to do their own work—and giving them the tools and support to do it. It means talking and listening and cheering on the child, as well as providing a (figurative) kick in the pants when warranted. It means your child will face frustrations that seem unfair but offer yet another chance to grow. It means you (and other adults) will have to be strong enough to allow your child to experience, and gain from, the hurts as well as the joys. This is real life. Your kid will benefit more from being supported and guided through it than being sheltered and excused from it.

All the skills mentioned are necessary for all children, regardless of the presence of disability. But kids with disabilities need additional knowledge of themselves to negotiate a world that tends not to value their differences. They need opportunities and support to practice applying their skills while they are growing up, so when they reach adulthood they will be well equipped to take on their own lives.

∾

PAT DANIELSON *lives in North Dakota with her two cats, Dexter and Serena Rose, and a foster dog, PGII. She is actively involved with her niece and nephews, providing resources for their disability needs and respite for her sister. Pat also helps care for her elderly parents. An advocate for the civil rights of people with disabilities, she testifies at the state capitol and writes letters concerning legislation. She has worked on the board of directors for Options Center for Independent Living and is a past president of the North Dakota Statewide Independent Living Council. Pat's experience as a child with juvenile rheumatoid arthritis taught her the value of starting early to teach children with disabilities how to be their best selves.*

Pat holds a B.S. in Education from the University of Missouri at Columbia. She loves telling everyday stories of people and aspires to be a published nonfiction author.

WHAT I'D TELL THAT DOCTOR

Jason Kingsley

I AM JASON KINGSLEY. I am now almost twenty-nine years old. Ten years ago I wrote an article for *Count Us In: Growing Up with Down Syndrome* (Harcourt Brace & Company, 1994), a book that Mitchell Levitz and I wrote. That article is about a confrontation I would have had with the obstetrician—if I had met him—about what he said years ago to my parents when I was born.

What I would say to the obstetrician is the same as what I would say to the parents of any newborn child who is born with a disability and who is born with Down syndrome.

The things I said ten years ago are true now and even more so.

When I wrote that article, I was still in school. But now I am on my own. I live in a house with two other roommates. We have very little supervision. We do our own cooking; we do our own shopping and cleaning. We do take public transportation. And above all else, our house is accessible to the community and to our work.

All three of us work in the community. I happen to work in the White Plains (New York) Public Library. My roommate Raymond works at PETCO, a pet store, and has been there for six years. And Yaniv works at an Armonk (New York) law firm.

In conclusion, I hope you will look at this article that I wrote ten years ago. Then get *Count Us In: Growing Up with Down Syndrome* and read the whole thing. You will find it very essential, inspiring, and helpful.

Here is my article:

WHEN I WAS BORN, the obstetrician said that I cannot learn, never see my mom and dad and never learn anything and send me to an institution. Which I think it was wrong.

Today we were talking about if I could see my obstetrician and talk to him, here are things I would say . . .

I would say, "People with disabilities *can learn*!"

Then I would tell the obstetrician how smart I am. Like learning new languages, going to other foreign nations, going to teen groups and teen parties, going to cast parties, becoming independent, being . . . a lighting board operator, an actor, the backstage crew. I would talk about history, math, English, algebra, business math, global studies. One thing I forgot to tell the obstetrician is I plan to get a academic diploma when I pass my RCTs* . . .

I performed in "The Fall Guy" and even wrote this book! He never imagined how I could write a book! I will send him a copy . . . so he'll know.

I will tell him that I play the violin, that I make relationships with other people, I make oil paintings, I play the piano, I can sing, I am competing in sports, in the drama group, that I have many friends, and I have a full life.

So I want the obstetrician will never say that to any parent to have a baby with a disability any more. If you send a baby with a disability to an institution, the baby will miss all the opportunities to grow and to learn . . . and also to receive a diploma. The baby will miss relationships and love and independent living skills. Give a baby with a disability a chance to grow a full life. To experience a half-full glass instead of the half-empty glass. And think of your abilities not your disability.

---

*New York State Regents Competency Tests

I am glad that we didn't listen to the obstetrician. . . . We will send a copy of this book to [him] and say, "See page 27." I wonder what he will say. I wonder if he will come to us and call us and what is his response, and we hope he would say that he made a mistake. His emotional feelings is . . . sorry, depressed, and mistaken. . . . He will never discriminate with people with disabilities again.

And then he will be a better doctor.

~

JASON KINGSLEY *is thirty years old and has Down syndrome. Jason graduated from Lakeland High School in Shrub Oak, New York, with an academic diploma, having passed all New York State Regents Competency Tests.*

Jason has appeared in many television shows including "Sesame Street," a starring role in "The Fall Guy" when he was ten years old, and a guest appearance on "Touched by an Angel." His other hobbies include oil painting, playing the piano and violin, and running the lighting board for a local community theater group.

Along with his lifelong friend Mitchell Levitz, Jason coauthored a book called Count Us In: Growing Up with Down Syndrome. *It is currently in its fourth printing.*

Jason works at the White Plains (NY) Public Library in the Video Department and lives independently in a house in Hartsdale (NY) with two roommates.

PLEASE BELIEVE ME

Tamra Garner

MY DISABILITY DOES NOT SHOW.
But it is still there.

Please believe me.

When I was young, I really was sick. I loved school and would not fake illness to get out of class.

I was a high achieving first child and succeeded in school and other activities only because of stubborn self-determination.

I fell asleep on the school bus halfway home because I was so exhausted, not because I was antisocial.

I could not sit up at a table or desk to do my homework because I was so weak at the end of each day.

I felt like fainting every time I bent over.

I needed times to rest throughout the day. I could not go on, I was shaking so hard.

I had severe headaches when I spent even twenty minutes in the sun.

I hurt severely when touched, even in play.

I was skinny because I could not absorb nutrients from my food, not because I didn't like supper.

I retreated, or self-protected, when the pain was unbearable. I did not dislike those around me.

I needed you to believe me then.

I need you to believe me now.
My disability does not show.
But it is still there.
Believe me.

~

TAMRA GARNER *spent her childhood years on the family wheat farm
north of Denver, Colorado. When she was a preteen, it was discovered that the home's well water had been poisoned by organophos-
phates, nerve gas components, mustard gas components, fluoride
ninety times the level of rat poison, and numerous other agents. Tamra
became ill with progressive health problems that remained undiagnosed for almost thirty years.*

*Tamra worked as site coordinator/workshop presenter for state
and federal research grants for high-risk families, before being permanently disabled with four autoimmune conditions in 1999. One of
the benefits, as well as the banes, of these conditions is that her
appearance is normal. Her function definitely is not.*

*Tamra now lives with her family in a high mountain valley in
southern Colorado.*

PARENTS WITHOUT PREJUDICE

Gregor Wolbring

THE FOLLOWING QUOTATION about thalidomide children and their families is from *Dark Remedy: The Impact of Thalidomide* written by T. Stephens and R. Brynner (Perseus Publishing, 2001). This quotation illustrates the attitudes of society that my parents and I faced.

> How did parents endure the shock [the birth of a thalidomide baby]? The few who made it through without enormous collateral damage to their lives had to summon up the same enormous reserves of courage and devotion that are necessary to all parents of children with special needs and disabilities; then, perhaps, they needed still more courage, because of the special, peculiar horror that the sight of their children produced in even the most compassionate. Society does not reward such courage because what those parents experience represents our own worst nightmare, ever since we first imagined becoming parents ourselves. The impact upon the brothers and sisters of the newborn was no less horrific. This was the defining ordeal of their family life—leaving aside for now the crushing burden on their financial resources from now on. (pages 65–66)

Public perception was that parents of thalidomiders had it very hard because their kids were indeed seen as monsters. In some ways, this reaction was understandable as the visible physical differences were similar to people coming back from wars without legs or arms. And, society's views about war and war veterans have often been quite negative. In addition, there is a basic societal understanding about how humans perform everyday tasks using their arms and legs. As a result, it remains difficult for people to accept individuals who eat with their feet and use crawling, rather than walking, to get around. People are expected to walk on their own two feet.

It is not surprising that public discussion of selective abortion and euthanasia/mercy killing surged after the publicity that followed the birth of thalidomide babies. At the time, it was commonly believed that thalidomiders were better off dead because they were suffering a great deal and would never be able to enjoy life.

My parents encountered these prejudices by neighbors and relatives as well as society at large. And, being brought up within society, many parents of thalidomiders were prone to feel the same prejudices themselves.

But I was lucky. My parents never had such prejudices. They accepted me as I was. Despite my look and the inability to look back in history and see what people like me could achieve, my parents accepted me—even through the difficult experiences they had with me during my hospitalizations as an infant and young child.

Furthermore, my parents were strong enough to reject modifications to my body proposed by medical professionals, such as cutting off my feet, which would be irreversible and seemed to serve no purpose. They did accept artificial legs for me—which they saw as useful. However, they did not stand in the way when I decided, later on in life, that I'd rather not use them. This was made possible by the fact that these legs were add-ons, which could be removed easily.

My parents were not rich or otherwise special, except that they were without prejudice and did not impose certain expectations on their kids. Whatever we were, we were. They also did not expect their children to be tools to serve their desires and needs.

Thanks to their love and acceptance, I developed high self-esteem and was able to become comfortable with my nonmainstream body and with who I am. I was able to develop my movements and other adaptations that I felt were useful for me. I never felt ashamed about crawling. For me, it was and still is, my natural way of moving.

With my self-esteem, I was able to take on the bullies of the world and disregard them for what they are. I never felt I had to prove myself to them, and I never saw myself as defective. My parents always helped me to look at the bigger picture. They made me aware that I was not the only one bullies would target. They enabled me to cope with the bad treatment I sometimes received.

My self-esteem has come in handy in many stages of my life. Without my high self-esteem, I would have never tried to become a biochemist or ventured into disability politics to try to help other people with disabilities and their relatives and friends. Professionally, I would not be fighting for a disability rights approach within the field of bioethics.

When I was fourteen, the school in my hometown was moved into a wheelchair inaccessible new building. When this happened, my parents and I decided to find an accessible mainstream school. But, the one we found was too far away from home for a daily commute. As a result, each night, I stayed at an institution for people with disabilities in the same town as the mainstream school—until I was twenty. At the institution, the residents were treated as defective people and expected to be thankful for everything that was done for them. Without my self-esteem, I would not have survived that institution and been prepared to confront the prejudices of the world.

My self-esteem had evolved during my first fourteen years with my parents. I had learned that I had rights as a person and that I was not defective. I also learned two important perspectives from my parents: to not get hung up on people who treated me badly, or take such treatment personally; and, to focus on those individuals who were kind, nice friends. Living by this outlook themselves, my parents were able to ignore the prejudiced people and to enjoy their many friends and relatives. And, the majority of my parents' friends and relatives accepted me as I am.

As I grew older, I developed my own relationships with some of my parents' friends and relatives. Friendship is important to me. I am still in contact with people from elementary school and from other times when I developed friendships.

My parents also taught me that I have a responsibility to do my share against prejudice. If they hadn't seen past public perception and prejudice, I wouldn't be where I am today. I now appreciate how lucky I was to have been raised by my parents.

To bring the story full circle, and in contradiction to the quote with which I started this essay, I was never the monster and I did not destroy the lives of my parents or younger sister. Society was, and often still is, the monster. Society's unwillingness to accept and support the diversity of human beings is the major threat to the well-being of people with disabilities and their families. Children and adults with disabilities are not the threats. My parents are not worse off because of me. In fact, they have said that I helped them have a better life because they focused on the key issues in life—friends, acceptance, and being human.

~

GREGOR WOLBRING *is a thalidomider, born in Germany. He studied biochemistry at the University College London, United Kingdom, and at the University of Tuebingen, Germany. He received his doctorate at the University of Frankfurt working under Nobel Laureate Prof. Hartmut Michel at the Max Planck Institute for Biophysics. He is currently a biochemist at the University of Calgary in Canada and an adjunct professor of bioethics at the University of Alberta and the University of Calgary, both in Canada.*

In addition, Gregor is the executive director and founder of the International Center for Bioethics, Culture, and Disability and the coordinator and founder of the International Network on Bioethics and Disability. He serves on the boards of many groups, including the Canadian Commission for UNESCO, the Canadian Center for Disability Studies, and the Action Group on Erosion, Technology, and Concentration (ETC, USA).

THE VIRTUES OF "BALLPARK NORMALCY"

Lisa Blumberg

WHEN A CHILD IS FIRST LABELED as having a disability—and somehow it is always a doctor who does the labeling, the diagnosing—the first question that parents ask is, "Will she have a normal life?"

The doctor will usually answer by discussing the aspects of the child's condition he thinks can be changed and those he thinks cannot be. Parents are left with the belief that the way to achieve the normal life they want for their child is to do everything they can to minimize the child's disability. This will be so whether the child's disability is physical, sensory, or cognitive. Parents will pursue early intervention, technology, and surgery—whatever it takes. However, this type of all-or-nothing approach may end up causing everyone's life to be more abnormal than accepting aspects of a child's disability.

As a person born with a physical disability resulting from athetoid cerebral palsy, I wish that someone would tell parents about the virtues of ballpark normalcy. *Ballpark normalcy* refers to a life that is not quite normal—but is "in the ballpark." This type of life is a little harder than a normal life. It is also a little better because one has the heightened perception and quirky insight that comes from being on the circumference of the mainstream.

Ballpark normalcy is about self-esteem and taking pleasure in one's own interests, whether it be collecting magnets, which I like to do, or reading books by Anne Tyler, which I also like to do. It is being an individual first and being a person with a disability perhaps fourth or seventh, depending on the situation one is in at the time.

How does ballpark normalcy play out in practical terms? When parents allow their four-year-old who can hardly stand to have his birthday party at a gymnastic center because that is where he says he wants to have it, they are doing the right thing. Part participant and part observer, rolling over and over while his friends jump and leap, the birthday boy is thrilled. The parents may feel some sadness but it is only *their* sadness. Their son is doing what he wants to do— and is in the ballpark.

Parents need to appreciate that their view of disability may differ radically from their offspring's view. For parents, disability may be an unplanned surprise ("I didn't even know what it was"), a tragedy, touching and poignant. For the child, it may just be a given, something that is natural. Many people with disabilities of my generation are vaguely guilty that our parents felt so badly about the fact we were mobility impaired or whatever our disability happened to be. Hopefully, due to the pride engendered by the disability rights movement, this will be less of a concern for today's children.

A rule of thumb that parents should follow is that what is good for children without disabilities will generally be good for children with disabilities, and that what is bad for ordinary children will generally be bad for children with disabilities. If you believe that your ordinary children should have "downtime" after school, you should try to make sure your child with a disability also has downtime. If you don't think it would be productive to applaud your ordinary daughter every time she picks up a pencil or puts on her coat, don't overwhelm your daughter with a disability with praise every time she does these things.

I'll interject a personal note here: Excessive praise for doing something normal is not a spur to further achievement. Instead, it just makes a person feel like a freak.

If there is one thing that all children—with or without disabilities—have in common, it is that kids don't always do what parents
want. Your hearing son may not want to play on the soccer team you
helped organized. Your deaf son may sign like there's no tomorrow
but have no interest in oral speech. Neither son may want to take
over the family business. All parents need to come to terms with
these facts of life. Incidentally, doctors and other professionals may
need to be reminded of the fact that kids don't always do what parents want. Too many of these folks don't seem to perceive that your
child may be rather like their child.

Speaking of doctors, they are useful in that they can sometimes
provide you with information you need or suggest approaches or
treatments that may benefit your child. However, never let any professional tell you what your goals or your child's goals should be.
Try to go to a physician who enjoys and appreciates your child. Find
someone who does not have all the answers because perhaps he or
she will ask the right questions.

Itzhak Perlman, the great concert violinist, learned to play the
violin as a child after becoming mobility impaired as a result of having polio. The world is lucky indeed that his parents let leg exercises
play second fiddle to music lessons. While in most cases, a person's
gifts may not be so clear, always remember that the way your child
can reach his or her potential may have nothing to do with mini-
mizing their disability. An hour of blowing bubbles may do more to
help your child become a happy, adjusted adult than an hour of
stretching.

Pursue your own interests, too. Don't feel you have to volunteer
for every disability-related cause you hear about if that's not your
style.

I must confess that I have interests and attitudes that I might not
have if I did not have a disability. This is part of ballpark normalcy.
For example, I do not have children myself. However, I know the
value of flexibility and innovation. This means that although I work
full-time in a company that sees 8 A.M. to 5 P.M. as the norm, I will
go to bat for any coworker who wants to work reduced hours to

have more time for family. Sometimes, my advocacy has made the crucial difference. This pleases me tremendously!

I am an aging baby boomer now. If there is one thing I have learned, it is that time goes by really fast. I know I have had some opportunities that I haven't made good use of, but I try to remain open to new things as they come my way. My key message to new parents, whether your child has a disability or not, is that you seize the day! Love your child. Enjoy your child. Respect your child. But, live the life you were meant to live. Your child, if she or he is lucky, will also live the life she or he was meant to live—or at least something in the ballpark.

~

LISA BLUMBERG *was born in the 1950s in Montclair, New Jersey, a wonderful place to grow up with three brothers and the family dogs. She attended local public and private schools and enjoyed the cultural opportunities in nearby New York City. When Lisa was sixteen, her family moved to Massachusetts. She graduated from Wellesley College in 1974 and from Harvard Law School in 1977.*

For over twenty years, Lisa has been an in-house corporate lawyer, first with Aetna and now with Travelers, both insurance companies. Her specialty is property/casualty law. In her "other" life, she has written more than twenty articles on medical ethics and disability rights topics. Lisa has also written about author Laura Ingalls Wilder and the historical basis of her "Little House" books. She has also served on the board of the Connecticut Women and Disability Network and has lectured to physical therapy students. For fun, she enjoys concerts, plays, and museums.

TAKE ME AS I AM!

Mark Enston

PARENTS! You cannot live with them; you cannot live without them. Parents have a hell of a task. And there is more bad news: there is no universally right or wrong way to deal with growing people.

Children with disabilities need to feel cool and need to be accepted by peers. All parents are embarrassing and old-fashioned to a growing youth, and children with disabilities feel this most keenly because their parents usually give them less freedom for independent interaction with their peers.

Guilt, sympathy, fear, and anger are some of the mixed emotions that are part of the melting pot in the relationship between a youth with a disability and a parent. These emotions spring from parental love, but that is not to say that it is always beneficial to the child with a disability. There is a seemingly innate need for parents to molly-coddle children and youths living with a disability. We do need some protection and caring—but we do not need it 24/7 in our faces.

Already I hear you saying that I am an ungrateful blind man with a pine forest on my shoulder. But I can assure you that I speak for nearly every young person with a disability whom I have met.

My own story is only one of thousands. But I believe it will reinforce my argument that most people living with a disability do not want or need to be overprotected by parents. I caught the flu when I was younger; it attacked my pancreas and knocked out a good portion of my insulin glands, leaving me with diabetes. The doctor pulled out a syringe—I nearly passed out—and he told me that I would be having one of these at least once a day for the rest of my life. It is all water off a duck's back to me now. But at that early age, this was a major trauma in my life and a constant source of embarrassment. Despite the fact that diabetes is fairly common in today's society, most people do not understand the condition or its implications.

At school, I would constantly hide the fact from my peers, especially girls, by eating sugary foods like every other kid. This was my attempt to be normal and accepted by my peers. But I had no idea of the lasting effects I would suffer by not adhering to a diabetic diet. I was a young musician playing in a band, and I was not going to allow a little diabetes to ruin my cool image. On canteen day at school, I would buy the chocolate milk drink and doughnuts that all the other kids bought for lunch. What would people say if I bought dry cracker biscuits, fruit, and water? Sometimes, when we were sneaking a cigarette behind the tennis courts, friends would ask me if they might catch diabetes if they shared a cigarette with me. Others would only know that I had something wrong with me, something to do with my blood or sugar. Political correctness prevented anybody asking directly about my condition and I was doing a credible job avoiding the issue—denial worked for me.

My parents plied me with sugarless everything, but it was embarrassing and tasted lousy. I would balk at bringing friends home because they would see my insulin syringes, and I would not be able to offer them a sweet biscuit or piece of chocolate cake. What sort of person would do that to their mates? When I was going out with friends, I dreaded my mother asking me if I had packed my needles and insulin. She would remind me not to eat anything too sweet while I was out. This made me feel that I was not like everybody else and destroyed my cool image by embarrassing me in front of friends.

I became interested in girls, as is the want of most teenage boys, and my denial became absolute. For twelve months, I dated the same girl and she never had an inkling that I was diabetic. I would have nightmares about her finding out about my condition, laughing at me, and walking away. My fear of rejection seems laughable with the hindsight that comes from age. But when you are a teenager, struggling to find an identity, embarrassment in front of your peers is a trauma that can prejudice self-esteem and social skills.

Parents must understand the need for their children to be accepted as one of the crowd. This is particularly so for kids living with a disability or medical condition. Parents need to keep a vigil for the well-being of their child with a disability, but we do not want to be smothered with care. We might need an elbow across a busy street or a push up a ramp, but this is what we ask you to accept: We may be a bit different to other kids, but let us forget about this and get on with life. Take us as we are!

Parents and society inculcate children with disabilities with fervent moral codes. People expect people with disabilities to be humble, conservative, thankful, and, worst of all, mega do-gooders. How boring! The disability community cannot be covered with any one blanket because we are a widely varied group from all sorts of social and cultural backgrounds. Do people with disabilities find it harder to pass through the gates of heaven than an able-bodied criminal?

Because of my diabetes, I lost my eyesight about ten years ago and started putting in more time with another of my passions. Writing has always been a constant delight and source of creative release, as is my music. At the age of sixteen, I read the Charles Dickens novel *Barnaby Rudge*. Stagg is a blind character who is the nastiest of the nasty because not only is he a blackmailer, he also has a disability. How dare he live outside the legal social codes! Stagg's blindness adds another dimension to his criminal nature. This is because of the high moral expectations placed upon the people with disabilities. I am not condoning unlawful behavior. But I believe a subversive or nonconformist nature in a person with a disability should be accepted—or otherwise—with the same judgment as that of an able-bodied person.

Have I no feeling for you, because I am blind? No, I have not. Why do
you expect me, being in darkness, to be better than men who have their
sight—why should you? Is the hand of Heaven more manifest in my having no eyes, than in your having two? It's the cant of you folks to be
horrified if a blind man robs, or lies, or steals; oh yes, it's far worse in
him, who can barely live on the few halfpence that are thrown to him
in streets, than in you, who can see, and work, and are not dependent
on the mercies of the world. A curse on you! You who have five senses
may be wicked at your pleasure; we who have four, and want the most
important, are to live and be moral on our affliction. (*Barnaby Rudge*,
page 289)

Writing nearly 150 years ago, Dickens had the perspicacity to
identify and address the high moral expectations shouldered by the
people with disabilities. Stagg is undoubtedly a transgressor of normal social codes, but his blindness should not automatically increase
his villainy.

My parents, professors, and editors often commend me on my
writing but suggest that I should write "nice" stories. I do not like
writing "feel good" fiction! I enjoy confrontational stories because
I believe that the shock factor often gets a message across with more
clarity than treading gently around sensitive topics. Parents should
encourage different thinking in their children with disabilities
because without change there can be no progress.

We ask that we be accepted as we are and then look further—to
discover our real differences. People living with disabilities are fat,
skinny, patient, grumpy, conservative, wacko, religious, naughty, and
any other characteristic you will find in a group of able-bodied persons. Our disability is only one of the many differences that make
up our identities.

The final icing to my argument comes from an experience I was
involved in during 1999. I was asked by our local blind association
to write and record a song with other musicians with disabilities—
to represent the needs and feelings of young persons with a disabil-

ity. Everybody in the group was asked to write some verses so that the song was representative of all of us. We cut the song as a CD, called ourselves Music Mania, and performed the song at dozens of events, including the Olympic flame ceremony in 2000. I was blown away when all the lyrics were put together. Everybody wrote about their desire to be accepted as they are so that we can get on with life. Take me as I am!

~

MARK ENSTON *is a blind author living with his two children, John and Anushka, in a coastal suburb of the world's most isolated city, Perth, Western Australia. Enston is in the final year of an English degree at Edith Cowan University and has had several magazine articles published as well as short stories. "Gorilla," a short story by Mark, is currently on the Malaysian TESL degree curriculum and was posted as the feature article on the U.S. website literatureclassics.com. He has won several small Australian literary and academic awards and plays music in a duo on weekends.*

Enston scans and reads anything that is not nailed down and uses talking books. He reads everything from Harry Potter to Dostoyevsky and even scans toilet paper if there is print on it. He enjoys the nearby beach and being driven crazy by his seven-year-old daughter and eighteen-year-old son.

PLEASE ACCEPT ME—ALL OF ME

Dianne Lotter

D EAR MOM AND DAD:
How I wish that you would have understood me while I was growing up. I believe I was always a very conscientious child, more sensitive to right and wrong than most children. I tended to be attuned to spirituality more than most children. I was more sensitive to the both of you—sensitive to the fact that you fought almost daily. I always stood in the background, listening but not understanding.

I always felt that I had a very upsetting time as a child. Both of you fought over every little thing. I remember often walking to school with tears coming down my face because I had just left the two of you fighting. It seemed to me that all you ever did was fight. I often asked you to get a divorce.

When I entered the convent at seventeen, you didn't want me to go. You wanted me to have a boyfriend and someday get married. But I chose to give my life to Christ. Then, when the convent asked me to leave because I exhibited extreme emotional disturbance, you made me promise to never tell anyone that I was asked to leave for such reasons. Sadly, at a very difficult time, life became even more difficult for me because I had to hide my shame. I certainly could have used some sympathy and understanding at that time of my life.

As time went on, my emotional problems became more severe. While going through college, I experienced some really bad times.

The psychologist I saw on a regular basis advised me not to go home on weekends because of the discord I met when I did go home. Once, when I was talking with you, Dad, you slapped me on the face really hard. Another time I was talking with you, and you got so mad at me you kicked me in the stomach. I always returned to college pretty messed up psychologically.

I didn't share any of this with you, mainly because mental illness was taboo for our "respectable" family. No one dared mention it. Your children were far too good for that. Years later, when my brother committed suicide the same held for him. We were guided away from talking about it. I had to keep all the grief within my darkened heart.

Life was a struggle for me as I entered more deeply into my adult life. My emotions were something I had to hide from you. When I was hospitalized and you both came to visit me, Dad, you yelled at me in the hospital bed. You told me to get up out of bed and stop acting like something was wrong with me. The nurses had to tell you to leave.

One time, when I was in the hospital for severe depression, you took me aside and told me about your marriage problems. I'm sorry, but I was too sick myself to give you any sympathy. Did you not realize that I loved both you and Mom and that any disagreements between the two of you were tearing me apart most of my young life?

Over the years, I was hospitalized many, many times for mental illness. I had over twenty psychiatrists throughout the years and about five psychologists, and many counselors, and other case-workers. My diagnosis was schizo-affective, manic-depressive. Through the years, it was very hard for me to come home and visit you both because you always made me feel that I had to hide my illness from the world. I always knew you were ashamed of me.

Of course, neither of you ever had a hint of mental illness. You always tried to decipher the mystery—where had my illness come from? Surely, not from either of you. This only made me feel worse, for I could never figure out where I had gotten it from. It must have been something I was to blame for myself. I certainly couldn't put the blame on either of you.

Now that I am grown and a grandmother, I still live with my illness. I still find it hard to talk about when I am with you because you deny it. You deny that any child of yours could be mentally ill. And you tell me how wonderfully I'm doing. Wouldn't it be nice if you could just look me straight in the eye and tell me how great a job I am doing surviving my illness? Wouldn't it be nice if you could pat me on the back, tell me that you know all I've been through, and that you recognize the good fight I've put up all my life? Wouldn't it be nice if you could admit that yes, your child was mentally ill; yes, your child was an alcoholic; and yes, your child attempted suicide many times? But no, you have to deny all of this because you don't have the inner strength to admit it. It would mean so much to me if you could accept me—all of me—and grasp the kind of life I have led, the sufferings I've gone through, and the strengths I have gained.

I would be afraid for you to read this letter. I would be fearful that you would be ashamed of me for writing so honestly about something I've lived with for sixty-two years. I've pretty well conquered my illness. I've learned to live a full life, to enjoy every moment I'm alive. I've lived to see my three daughters marry and to have grandchildren. I've learned to overcome my deep depression and to face life with certainty and honesty—to deal with life on life's terms.

It's a miracle that my daughters have done so well with their lives. It's amazing that I have two adorable little grandsons and beautiful twin granddaughters who just arrived. Now that I have a full, rich life, I look back and think it was all worth it—all the suffering, all the hospitalizations, all the mystery. I don't know how I got through it all.

I have developed a rich spiritual life, and it gives meaning to all the suffering I've borne. My spiritual life keeps me happy and joyful, and gives my life new meaning. I would be even more joy-filled if you could look at me, see the truth about me, and never again be ashamed of me.

I love you both very much. I know that you, Dad, are looking down at me from heaven. I believe that I love both of you very, very much. It was because I loved you both so much that I was hurt so severely by your constant fighting and bickering. If I hadn't loved you, nothing would have mattered to me. I wouldn't have suffered so much to see both of you suffering. But I know now that you couldn't help yourselves. You didn't have the help you needed at the time. I've learned to look back and forgive you—both of you.

I am learning to love you deeply and to realize how lucky I was to have parents who really loved me and cared about me. I forgive both of you for anything you might have done or said to hurt me. I beg your forgiveness for all the sorrow I have caused you in your lifetimes.

I have now found such joy in my life because there is no longer any shame. There is only a present and a future to be lived, one moment at a time.

There is a happy ending. Each moment of my life is now full and rich because I learned to love both of you—and I have also learned to love myself.

~

DIANNE LOTTER *is a college graduate with a B.A. in English and a minor in art. She is divorced with three daughters, all married. Her oldest daughter has two small boys, and her middle daughter has twin baby girls. Dianne's youngest daughter is married and is a nurse.*

Dianne is a Secular Carmelite, which defines her spirituality to an extent. She sees a psychiatrist on a regular basis and has a wonderful counselor, whom she sees every two weeks. While she needs medications, she lives a very symptom-free life, which she attributes to her deep spirituality. Dianne has many wonderful friends and never feels lonely, even though she lives alone in Wisconsin. Her hobbies keep her busy—she plays the organ and loves to read and write poetry.

2

PARENTS ARE
THE MOST
IMPORTANT EXPERTS

WHAT'S A MOTHER TO DO?

Cathy Putze

THANKS, MOM—for bringing me into this world. You chose to value my life rather than eliminate it just because I'm not what you expected. You expected a baby with all its parts in working order. Unfortunately, mine don't exactly jive.

I know you're wondering how on earth to hold a wiggle worm like me who stiffens unexpectedly. Your touch, the warm feeling of you, and being cradled in your arms will help me thrive. You are the person in this world I need to be able to make our journey together.

As you and Dad stand by my crib watching the involuntary movements of my eyelids as I sleep, it is natural to wonder if things will be OK. But trust that you have what it takes to get us through this. Sometimes, if you need to ask someone how to help me, don't be shy. A lot of guesswork lies ahead for both of us.

It's going to be hard for both of us to get used to the fact that I won't run as fast as others or talk as clearly. But that doesn't mean I'm helpless. I'll be able to do things, but I'm going to do them "my way."

When you take me to therapy and are asked to do exercises with me, please remember, I'm your child—not your client or patient. Just be my mom, not a therapist, educator, or doctor. I'll have plenty of those. I need a "mom" to hold me and reassure me on days when things don't go so smoothly.

Professionals, friends, relatives, teachers—almost everyone we meet—will have an opinion about how you should help me. Always remember, you are the one who lives with me twenty-four hours a day and sees what I can and cannot do. Don't be afraid to speak up and say what you think. Of all the opinions out there, yours is the one that counts the most.

Mom, how you feel about me is so important. How you feel about the disabilities I have is even more important. Do you agree or disagree with the negative things others say about children with disabilities? Do you see yourself as less of a mom because I'm not perfect? Do you feel overwhelmed and need help? Along with everyone else in our culture, you have been programmed to believe that a less than physically perfect child means failure and doom. The people who believe such things have not looked at themselves in a mirror and seen their own less than perfect images. You need to help me feel good about me even when the world outside my family does not give me positive messages. For your sake and mine, meet other folks like you and me who are taking the same journey. Let them help you so you can help me.

Every mom wants to protect her child. Because of my disabilities, you may want to protect me even more. But someday I will grow up and be on my own. I need all the training you can give me to do as much as I can for myself.

I need to know I'm a part of my family and not someone who takes away from the rest of the family. Please assign me a role in the family and give me chores to do. Show your confidence in me by letting me attempt things—even if you have to hold your breath while I do them.

Please tell my brother and sister about my disability and what can and cannot be done for me. After all, we're all in this together. When my eight-year-old brother asked what I had, you explained ever so gently that I was born with cerebral palsy and that it affected my muscles. And you assured him it wasn't anything he could catch.

Once, when he made me mad by eating my share of some cake, I wanted to donate my condition to him.

Sisters and brothers love and fight and make up. Having a disability will not stop me from getting involved. They may already be jealous because they think I get more attention than they do. Take time for them as well, and let them know you love us all. And, you don't need to take my side to protect me—just let us be a family.

I will also need times when I can be alone. Because so many people will be involved in our lives, our privacy as a family will be a concern. We all need times when we can be alone. I will also need free time with no responsibilities—just to be me. And I know that you will need some time for yourself as well.

Sometimes explaining who I am to others will be very hard. Some people who don't know anything about my disability will "freak out" or believe that I'm an "anathema." You and I are going to have to develop ways of dealing with such difficult scenarios.

I remember the day the first-grade teacher hit me for wetting my pants because she wouldn't excuse me from class to use the little girl's room. I really felt so ashamed, and all the kids laughed at me. They didn't know it wasn't my fault. You really blew your stack! Then you explained that I did not have the control over my bladder muscles others have. At the same time, you made it very clear to me that I better need to use the bathroom when I ask to be excused. Thanks for sticking up for me that day—and for educating my teacher and the other kids.

I wish you and Dad hadn't argued so much over whether I should have speech classes in school. Dad wanted me to be as normal as possible and downplayed my differences. You wanted me to have as much help as possible so I could be more like other children. It took a lot of guts to stand up and get me the help I needed. But it sure made me feel bad to know that I caused you and Dad to be mad at each other. Even though I was only six years old, if you had asked me, it would have made me feel like a "big girl." I would have told you that I didn't like being made fun of and wanted to learn to speak better. Later, when I grew up, I would decide I did as much as I could. This is the way I talk. You understand me, and that's that.

When my brother or sister did things I had trouble with, I began to learn I was different. I can remember how you laughed at my brother trying to take his first steps and how much encouragement you gave him. I remember how you held out your arms for joy when my sister walked toward you for the first time. I wondered how they brought you so much joy, and I seemed to make you cry when I began to walk. I didn't understand that your tears were tears of joy.

The road on this journey will be full of rough spots. We both have to just do what we can. There were many times I didn't understand your need to protect me. And, there were times I relished that protection because I was too scared to face the world apart from our family. There were times when you didn't understand my need to be with peers and not with family. We depended so much on each other. We both did the best we could.

I still have trouble understanding why some people don't want to be around me because of the way I look. I need to feel beautiful inside. One way I learn to like me is to know I am valued for who I am. Sadly, I've gotten many messages that say I'm not valued as a person. One time, a college peer told me she did not want me to go out with the group because she was uncomfortable with my cerebral palsy. I was able to tell her that's a poor excuse for excluding someone. But, the end result was I let that bully ruin an opportunity for friendships. You gave me the courage to stand up for myself and to believe in myself.

What's a mother to do? Be a parent in the best way you know how. I'll love you for it.

~

CATHY PUTZE *was born with cerebral palsy and a significant hearing impairment. Her childhood was spent in a Pennsylvania suburb with her parents, one sister, and one brother. Her parents encouraged learning, so she eventually graduated with a B.A. in psychology and later a master's degree in social work. In 1973 Cathy met and married her husband and they moved to Arizona.*

Cathy loves animals and has two dogs and a cat with an attitude. Her hobbies are malling, sewing, quilting, and simple organ playing, especially gospel music. She has been a strong advocate for people with disabilities and works hard for the right of everyone to be free to be a citizen of this land and to be in charge of their own lives.

THE RULES OF THE "GAME"

Jeff Moyer

WHEN I WAS FIVE YEARS OLD, two events visited my family that changed us forever. We lived in a working-class neighborhood in Cleveland, Ohio, and our family life was extraordinarily normal. Then, in July 1954, I contracted a severe case of measles that apparently triggered a genetic predisposition for a form of retinitis pigmentosa, resulting in slowly progressive blindness. That same summer, my brother, Mark, was born with a severe cognitive disability.

I remember the anticipation of Mark's birth and the night my grandmother arrived to take care of us while my parents rushed to the hospital. My father returned in the morning, grim and withdrawn. My mother and brother arrived some days later. My devastated mother sadly explained that my brother was different, that he had a condition then called mental retardation.

At the same time, my own life was changing drastically with the onset of vision loss. At first, my circumstance was not taken seriously. An optometrist told my parents that I was pretending that I couldn't see.

Based on my own experiences, the disability and life of my brother, and my work with families who have children with many other disabilities, I suggest five rules for parents and families.

Rule One: Trust your perceptions and observations of your child's abilities and disabilities. You are the best expert possible concerning your child. Your firsthand experience and in-depth knowledge are critical components in the diagnosis and understanding of any disability.

For three years, I lived with my parents and teachers insisting that I could see because of the opinion of one clinician. Oddly enough, because all the adults in my life believed that I was pretending I couldn't see, I had to pretend that I could—a difficult and confusing reality.

Rule Two: Talk to your children about their life experiences, and draw out and affirm their feelings. Once my vision loss had been taken seriously, a specialist saw me every six months. I well remember the dread of those visits—not because I would be told that my vision continued to deteriorate, but because my mother would be told and I knew how hard it was on her. As we drove home each time, she would announce that the doctor had said that I was continuing to go blind. Nothing else was ever said about the process.

I would have welcomed someone asking me how it was for me. During my slow, steady decline, some support for my emotional reactions would have helped. Like all losses, progressive losses can be processed. But it takes intentional and ongoing attention to do that psychological and emotional work.

By the time I was eleven, my vision had deteriorated to the point that I was moved to another school district with a class for kids with blindness and low vision. That poor Braille teacher! I refused to touch the dots since I could still see them with my face pressed to the page. The summer before, I had broken my nose trying to catch a baseball I couldn't see. If only someone had said that losing vision was scary and that I had every right to feel afraid and very sad. I might have been counseled that the fear and sadness would pass and that I could live a regular life regardless of how much I could see or

not. But, since there was no counseling—or any discussion at all—
I buried my feelings and clearly did not behave in my own best
interest.

Rule Three: Advocate! From birth, my brother began to show the
developmental disability with which he was born. Year after year,
he fell further behind his typically developing peers. My parents half-
heartedly advocated for him, but there were no legal protections in
those days. Time after time, preschools flatly stated, "Not him, not
here." Today, given our scope of legal protections, advocacy seems
to be the common denominator among families with kids who succeed in becoming integrated and achieve their individual potential.

   When Mark was eight, there were no schools that would accept
him and my mother and father made the heartbreaking decision to
institutionalize him. He was sent to live in a crowded and hopeless
prisonlike setting—an eventuality that broke my parents' hearts once
and for all. The compounded losses that my parents endured, and
the emotional devastation that resulted, never cleared. It hung like
a pall over our home, and, to numb their pain, my parents lost themselves in alcohol nightly.

Rule Four: Feel your losses fully and process them on an ongoing
basis. Disability is not tragedy; rather, it is a normal circumstance
in the human condition. However, having a child with a disability is
a profound loss because we lose our dreams of normalcy. In order
to release the difficult negative feelings, we must recognize the feelings, find our own best ways to express them, and then release them.
I don't think my parents ever fully released their feelings and the
resulting emotional toxicity eventually destroyed them.

   I have known many families with children who have complex,
and even multiple, disabilities who live joyfully and with humor,
optimism, and a deep appreciation for the beauty of their children.
They are also the families that process their feelings fully in many
ways, including with counseling, writing, networking with other

parents, family and pastoral supports, humor, and, almost always, a deeply grounded belief system.

All losses are the same in their emotional impact. I do understand about loss. Progressive blindness has been a long road and a stiff climb. But, as human beings, we can feel and release the difficult feelings and clear our emotional channel for the joy, humor, compassion, and optimism that are bludgeoned by anger and sadness. Advocacy propels a life worth living. My parents did not advocate and lived with the tragic results.

More than twenty years ago, I accepted my responsibility as my brother's advocate. Advocacy requires knowledge, tact, perseverance, support, passion, and gritty determination. In a series of five stages, I have successfully moved my brother from the worst possible institution imaginable to a comfortable suburban home where he now lives with supported living services.

Today, Mark and I live in the same neighborhood. We each enjoy a satisfying life that is different from the norm and different from each other. Mark continues to be one of my best teachers. Despite languishing for thirty-three years in terrible circumstances, Mark is the most forgiving, gentle, generous, and loving man I know.

Rule Five: Acceptance is a requirement for happiness. By acceptance, I do not mean a numb resignation, but rather, a deep, openhanded, and openhearted acceptance. I do not wish to change Mark, nor my own blindness. I truly believe that every life is worth living and that our fundamental equality as human beings springs from the deeper meaning of our common humanity.

Long after I had become a successful adult, my mother told me that she carried two burdens in her life—my brother and me. I was stunned to be considered a source of suffering when I consider myself a source of joy, hope, and goodwill. What my mother was really saying, I believe, was that she had never really grieved her losses. There is no greater pain than that which we feel for the suffering of our children. But today, neither Mark nor I suffer. We celebrate our love, enjoy frequent meals together, gather for every holiday, and maintain a strong and abiding family bond.

There is still much work to do to develop equal education, employment, and integrated community opportunities for individuals with disabilities. Every family who joins the ranks of those with disabilities has the opportunity to educate the uninitiated and work as social change agents. Together, we are truly changing the world and there is no more open or welcoming community than ours.

Each and every parent shapes the life of their child and, in turn, the future of the community into which they will grow. It has been said every functional family is functional in the same ways and every dysfunctional family is dysfunctional in its own unique way. Beyond the goals of individual accomplishment, disability offers a multiplicity of benefits to all who engage positively within the family. Patience, compassion, empathy, self-understanding, and many other benefits will be derived by the parents and siblings who embrace the opportunities life presents.

∼

JEFF MOYER *is a disability rights advocate, songwriter, author, and National Public Radio commentator living in Cleveland, Ohio. Jeff serves as an adjunct faculty member at Kent State University and has worked in many professional roles throughout his career. Perhaps Jeff is best known through his numerous CDs of original music that promote a positive attitude about disability in the context of normal human diversity. Jeff has presented and performed in forty-six states as well as internationally and his books and CDs are at work in homes, schools, and communities worldwide. His perspective is drawn from his own experience with progressive blindness, his brother's lifetime with severe cognitive disability, and his son's experience with attention deficit hyperactivity disorder (ADHD). Jeff also has an adult daughter and lives with his wife, Maggie.*

"DEAF PEOPLE CAN DO ANYTHING BUT HEAR"

Christina M. Pean

A S A YOUNG CHILD, I was fascinated with television shows such as "Romper Room," "Banana Splits," "Captain Kangaroo," and "Sesame Street." Those programs were a big part of my world prior to losing my hearing when I was three. Spinal meningitis left me unable to appreciate the shows that had become a part of my daily routine. My parents knew something was terribly wrong when I told them that the television repairman needed to come in because the sound was "broken."

I was outfitted with body aids, a cumbersome version of today's behind-the-ear hearing aids. The mammoth hearing aids did nothing for me. Even with those aids, I was not able to pick up environmental sounds. My parents finally gave up trying to get a hearing aid for me after two "disappeared." I am not quite sure what happened with the first one, but I know that the second hearing aid was collected on garbage day.

My parents came to the conclusion that they needed to teach me to maximize my other senses. My family practiced inclusion long before the word came into common usage. One of the first things my parents did was learn sign language. My siblings and I, in turn, picked it up. Between my speech-reading skills and snippets of information provided by my siblings, I was able to know what was going on.

My parents, both of whom were very involved when I was a student at the Illinois School for the Deaf, struck up friendships with administrators and educators at the school. The superintendent who was hard of hearing utilized sign language. Many of the professionals I came into contact with were able to sign. These persons had varying degrees of hearing loss.

In sign language, my father would engage in shoptalk with fellow administrators who worked within the state of Illinois. I watched two administrators expound upon the problems with the labor force and discuss day-to-day operations. I also remember going to events where deaf and hearing professionals mingled. The information I gleaned from those gatherings helped shape my future career plans. Upon learning that many of these deaf professionals graduated from Gallaudet University in Washington, D.C., my post-secondary plans were formulated. At the young age of ten, I decided to attend Gallaudet and find a field where I could make a difference in the lives of others.

I was aware that deaf people could talk on the telephone using a TTY (teletypewriter). My parents had one of those "old-fashioned" TTYs. It was a two-part unit. The part containing the keyboard was so heavy that two men were needed to carry it inside. A smaller unit contained the acoustic cups—where the telephone would go when a call came through on the TTY.

I do not remember using that particular model because it was rather difficult to use. When the smaller, portable TTYs first came out, my parents rented one from the telephone company. With this accessibility came a greater degree of independence. It became possible for me to call my folks from a TTY anywhere in town to let them know where I was and when I'd be home. Like my hearing siblings, I made calls to my peers. I would type sweet nothings to my boyfriend and weep when he telephoned to break up. When I went off to college, my parents kept the TTY so I could call home, just as my brothers and sisters did.

My siblings taught me about "listening in." Every now and then, the telltale phone cord led from a closet—with my brother nowhere in sight. My sister and I would quietly sneak upstairs and listen in on the extension. Between muffled giggles, my sister would tell me that he was on the phone with a girl. Unfortunately, we never were able to listen in on an entire conversation as my brother would say: "Get off the #!@* phone!"

In our family, adult conversations were rarely immune from prying ears and eyes. Since the heat vent carried kitchen sounds to an upstairs bedroom, my brothers and sisters would go upstairs and listen to conversations in the kitchen. I was allowed to stay in the kitchen until I made the fatal mistake of expressing my thoughts during one such discussion between my parents. With the realization I was able to speech-read quite well, I was sent out of the kitchen. This was disappointing, but not a problem. I just joined my siblings.

My brothers and sisters would share words from their favorite songs, tell me jokes they heard at school, and let me read stuff they brought home. They told me about events at their school (which usually involved Sister X and/or Monsignor). When my school made it to the regional basketball tournament, they shared game highlights and scores that were transmitted over the radio.

In the days before the term *closed-captioning* was coined, my family would interpret my favorite shows. Interpreting is much harder than it appears. The interpreter must be able to listen to and retain the information that is being transmitted. As this information is shared with a deaf person, more information will continue to come through. Interpreting often requires "judgment calls" when the interpreter needs to decide how to best convey the material. One can be either a participant or an interpreter; the two are not inclusive.

My siblings would interpret "Little House on the Prairie" for me each week. This included reruns (which they had already interpreted before). For one hour each week, they gave up an hour of their time to interpret this show. When Sears sold the first decoder, my parents saw to it that we got one so that we could all enjoy television together. To this day, my siblings groan at the thought of interpreting "Little House." They, too, appreciate the convenience and access that closed-captioning provides.

Many misconceptions occur when a person has a disability. I saw my siblings spring to my defense time after time. When a young child heard my "deaf" voice and ran away in terror, my family let me know that the problem was ignorance—it was not something I had done. I was encouraged to use my talents to combat ignorance. I did this by writing poetry. One such poem was entitled: "Just like you . . . (except in one small sense). . . . "

After thirteen years as a day student at the Illinois School for the Deaf, I went to Gallaudet University. I was able to communicate directly with my professors, advisors, and other staff using sign language. Since all buildings had fire alarms with strobe lights, an alarm would turn the entire building into a discotheque. A student could make room occupants aware of her or his visit by flicking a switch. This motion would cause the room lights to flash until the door was answered or the visitor left. Activities off-campus were never a problem because the Washington metro area had an excellent pool of qualified sign language interpreters.

In my junior year, the Gallaudet Board of Trustees conducted a nationwide search for a president. The pool of candidates was narrowed down to three qualified finalists, two of whom had a hearing impairment. Letters, telegraphs, and newspaper articles called for the appointment of a president with a hearing impairment. To the surprise and shock of many, someone with no hearing loss, or knowledge of the needs of individuals with a hearing loss, was selected. I was very much involved in the activities leading up to the election of Gallaudet's president and was on the front line of the Deaf President Now protest in 1988.

Much has been written about the student-led protest that resulted in the appointment of Gallaudet's first deaf president, Dr. I. King Jordan. This movement attracted the attention of politicians on both sides of the aisle, persons in television and film, and national disability groups as well as the media all over the world. Upon his selection, Dr. Jordan declared, "Deaf people can do anything but hear."

This may be a novel concept for people who do not know about the untapped talents that exist within persons with disabilities. Not so for my parents and siblings. More than twenty years before Dr. Jordan's famous remark, they taught me that self-imposed limitations were the only ones that I needed to accept.

≈

CHRISTINA PEAN *had a bout with spinal meningitis at the age of three that left her profoundly deaf and blind in one eye. After graduating from the Illinois School for the Deaf, she attended Gallaudet University in Washington, D.C., and graduated cum laude in 1989. She received a master's degree from the University of Maryland in 1993.*

As a student volunteer at Gallaudet University, Christina was involved with the planning and implementation of Deaf Way I, an international festival that drew individuals from seventy countries in the world. Subsequent to that experience, she traveled through the former U.S.S.R. and lived in Orleans, France, for a year.

Christina works as a Program Specialist in the division of Services to Persons Who Are Deaf and Hard of Hearing (SDHH) in the Illinois Department of Human Services/Office of Rehabilitation Services.

THE AUTISM BOMB

Stephen Shore

Y OUR CHILD HAS JUST been diagnosed with a disability. Could it be? Perhaps the doctor is wrong. No, not us! We don't have these types of problems in our family.

Uncle Bill is very quiet, doesn't like crowds of people, and is fine as long as everything is in its place. . . . What will our parents say? Whose side of the family did this come from?

OK—our child has a disability. Now, how can we cure our child? Will our child be able to walk, talk, have friends, work, marry, and lead a normal life? What is "normal" anyway?

Your child is the same child after the label is given. Why is there such a feeling of loss and mourning? Is it really about our child or perhaps a sadness about the preconceived goals and aspirations for our child that now seem impossible?

There is so little information out there. Or, maybe it goes the other way—there are reams of material about this new status our child has been given. Books, pamphlets, support groups, Internet, and even adults with this disability talking about it at conferences. Wow! This is too much. What is the right way to work with *our* child? Information overload! Where do we turn?

In 1961, a child was born after only two hours of easy labor. He started turning over at eight days of age. Nothing is wrong with *this* child. For this child, there was rapid physical development. Speech and other developmental milestones were passed with flying colors. Everything was rolling along quite nicely until about eighteen months of age.

And then . . . withdrawal from the environment, loss of speech, tantrums, screaming, spinning in circles, and self-abusive behavior. What happened? Must have been something Mother did. She remembers being quite annoyed with and yelling at the older sibling while nursing the younger baby. Ah—that's it. Or, was it mental retardation? After all, his older sibling was diagnosed with mental retardation. No—this is different. The word *autism* spills out of the family pediatrician's lips. He wasn't sure—but this warranted attention by some specialists.

The diagnosis was made by a team of professionals at a school for children with disabilities. "Atypical Development, Strong Autistic Tendencies, and Psychotic." Why not throw in the kitchen sink, too? "Listen," said the professionals. "You have your marriage and two other children to take care of. We know of specially trained people who can take care of and teach your child. Why don't we send your child to . . ."

The parents refused to let the child be taken away from the home that provided love and security. With much force and conviction, they convinced the school to take the child as a day student in a year, when it had more room. Perhaps the child will outgrow this disability. The parents accepted their child for who he was.

The autism bomb had hit and it hit hard. I was the child diagnosed with "Atypical Development, Strong Autistic Tendencies, and Psychotic." Not that dealing with any disability is simple, but things are easier today than they were almost forty years ago when my parents received my diagnosis. Today, there is much hope for a bright future and fulfilling lives for people with disabilities.

My parents have had the greatest effect on my success in leading a fulfilling and productive life in education, work, and marriage. Earning this success has been hard work along the way. I often doubted whether I would be able to accomplish my goals. My parents were the ones who saw a child with intelligence and possibilities. Instead of focusing on the disorder, my parents saw my condition as a different order of being. I believe that it would be better to look at all of what is considered a disability as a different order of being. I think of these different orders of being as "*diff*abilities," a set of strengths and weaknesses that vary from what society deems as typical and necessary in order to achieve success. My parents said "no" to institutionalization and "yes" to early intervention. My parents accepted me for who I was and didn't try to cure me.

The term *early intervention* had not actually been coined in my parents' day. They just did what parents do for a child that has needs. Put into today's terms, my parents' efforts could be considered as an early intervention program emphasizing music, movement, sensory integration, and narration.

Children with autism are born with a set of scrambled sensory receivers. Some senses are turned up too high whereas others are turned down too low. In addition to these issues of "volume control," the information that comes in may be distorted. I believe this is also true of many children with other cognitive disabilities.

Today, parents are encouraged to use "narration" to develop understanding and communication. The idea of narration is to provide an enthusiastic, running commentary of a child's activities as they take place. It is an interesting and very useful technique that replaces the ubiquitous "Good Job!" that is usually too abstract for young children who tend to live in the here and now. Hopefully, with the running commentary of a child's activities, the child eventually attaches these words to the action he or she is doing. Anyone working with a child can narrate with excitement. For example, a child hanging cups on hooks will hear an enthusiastic, running commentary on what is being done, "Stephen is hanging cups on hooks," rather than "Good job!"

My mother would try to get me to imitate her. That didn't work. She then imitated me. I suddenly became aware of her existence.

Once she became a part of my environment, we began to communicate. Imitating to get a child's attention is now a commonly used practice in teaching. The teacher meets the learner at his level before introducing new knowledge or understanding. Put bluntly: if you need to get down on the floor—or otherwise act in ways you might think are silly—in imitation of your child to get his or her attention, then that is what you do. The best teachers start where their students are familiar and use that as a base to bring them to the unfamiliar.

My mother did this at a time when there were no methods for working with children on with what is now called the "autism spectrum." She did what she felt was right—nothing more and nothing less. It is important to do what seems right for your child. At least in the field of autism, and I also suspect this is true for other disabilities. There is no one methodology or treatment that fits all situations.

My parents must have done some good because by the time I was admitted to the special school that originally recommended institutionalization, I was starting to speak. Another evaluation placed me as "neurotic" rather than "psychotic." Things were moving up in the world for me! With much hard work from my parents, friends, educators, and others, I am able to write this essay to you that I would have liked my parents to have when the dreaded "A" word landed and blew their world apart.

How can you make life better for your child with a different set of abilities?

Acceptance. Your child is the same child he or she was before the diagnosis. A diagnosis can mean access to needed educational and community services.

Professionals. You will come in contact with many professionals in the business of helping children. Help them help you. Make sure you have input in any decision making for your child. You are the expert on your child. And, since these people are often harried, overworked, and underpaid, make suggestions for improvements and express appreciation for a job well done when so warranted.

Community. There is a community of people with the same or similar condition. This community is accessible through the Internet, associations, and resource centers in your area as well as support groups, conferences, and more. With this community, you and your child or family will travel on a fascinating journey that may be different than you previously planned on, but at least as enriching and rewarding.

Stigma. This negative prejudging by others when they come in contact with your child of differing abilities can be defeated. All of us reading this book are charged with the responsibility of showing society that people with designated disabilities have the same needs, wants, and potential for a fulfilling life as everyone else.

It is the job of all of us to increase public awareness of the potential of all people of all abilities.

∼

DIAGNOSED WITH *"atypical development with strong autistic tendencies," Stephen Shore was viewed as "too sick" to be treated on an outpatient basis and recommended for institutionalization. Nonverbal until age four, with much help from his parents, teachers, and others, he is now completing his doctoral degree in Special Education at Boston University with a focus on helping people on the autism spectrum develop their capacities to the fullest.*

In addition to working with children and talking about life on the autism spectrum, Stephen presents and consults internationally on adult issues pertinent to relationships, employment, and disclosure as discussed in his book Beyond the Wall: Personal Experiences with Autism and Asperger Syndrome, *2nd ed. (Autism Asperger Publishing Company, 2003).*

Stephen serves on the board of the Autism Society of America and as board president of the Asperger's Association of New England. He is also on the boards of several organizations serving individuals with autism.

SOLUTIONS FROM THE HEART

Donna F. Smith

M Y CHALLENGE IN TELLING this story is to not make it one of those sappy articles on disability that I absolutely loath. But the fact is, I owe everything I have achieved as an adult to my mother's foresight and intuition in raising me to be as independent as possible. As the glory in this story is hers and not mine, perhaps I can attribute any sappiness to motherhood and her strength of character, rather than my disability.

I think the thing that awes me the most is that she made her decisions about disability, took her stand, and put them into action, years before the terms *inclusion*, *equal access*, and *civil rights* were applied to the disability community. She did what she did because she believed it to be right and ethical, and because in her endeavor to be the best mother she could be, she sought the path that would provide me with the most opportunities in life possible.

In 1960, Arlene was a young housewife, mother of four with a high school diploma, doing exactly what she had always wanted to do. The fact that her goal in life was to get married and raise children should in no way indicate that she was passive or lacked ambition. Nothing could be further from the truth. Competent, self-assured, and strong-willed, she threw herself, heart and soul, into creating a safe and happy home that focused on nurturing her four children, and any other children from the neighborhood who found their way into her mothering realm.

She did all the essentials to motherhood and being a housewife—she cooked, canned, cleaned, and sewed, and she spent volumes of time playing and teaching. She was smart enough to see to her own adult needs, too. She claimed her quiet time to read, pulled rank to watch her favorite shows on television, and sent us all to the babysitter's while she and my father entertained friends. But, her focus was most definitely the welfare of her children. All was not always rosy, either. She faced very adult struggles and concerns, but we didn't see any of that until much, much later in life.

About midway through 1960, Arlene was in her new three-bedroom ranch house on the outskirts of town, facing me, her youngest child, across a high-chair tray trying to convince me that I really did like strained peas and carrots. While making eye contact and funny faces to divert my attention from the odious task at hand, she noticed some unusual-looking spots near my pupils. Concerned, she made an appointment with the family ophthalmologist to have me checked out.

In a very short period of time, she learned that I had retinoblastoma, cancer of the retina, and that the prognosis was total blindness. Surgery was scheduled to remove the right eye, which was the most affected, and an extended schedule of treatments, an injection of a drug thought to be useful at that time, and radiation were arranged to treat the left eye. It was never assumed that such treatments would be successful in saving any vision. It was hoped that the treatments would be successful in stopping the tumors and saving the eye intact—in case future medical treatment might be able to restore vision.

For the next year and a half, Arlene's days were filled with a mixture of hope and anxiety—a mother's grief over anything that threatens one of her children and a fierce determination to see her child come out on top, even if she currently didn't fully know the challenges she faced. This was all complicated by a sobbing child who quickly learned the routine activities that led almost daily to painful injections in the arm and episodes with a very large and scary-looking machine. Further complicating the situation were the reactions of family and friends, which ranged from the minority reaction of "just tell us how we can help" to the majority reaction of fear, pity, and hysterical proclamations of offense against God.

She neither gave into the terror of her child or the overwhelming negativity of the uninformed and unwilling to learn. She reached deep within herself for the calm and balance that made her such a good mother, trusted her own basic instincts about what was right, and set about learning all she could regarding living with a person who is blind. Though she experienced in full measure the heart-breaking sorrow that a mother feels when something happens to her child that is beyond her control to stop, she also never doubted that I'd not only survive, but that I would not be diminished by it. She took it on, as her task as my mother, to help me find the best ways to cope and come out the winner.

One of her basic tenets in life is that whatever challenges we face make us stronger and better people for having faced them—facing disability was no different from any other life challenge. She was absolutely sure from the start that, although she would have given anything for me not to have to deal with blindness, now that it was inevitable, I would be a stronger, better person because of it.

She systematically rejected any notion that I would be inferior to other children, that there would be things in life I wouldn't be able to achieve or enjoy, or that lower standards and expectations would have to be set for me because I had a disability. She was bombarded with such sentiments from people who just assumed that such was understood by any rational person and that to expect greater of me was cruel and unrealistic. She became fiercer in protecting me against such negative influences than any tigress guarding her cubs. Her innate belief in my inalienable right to be allowed to have the chance to strive for all that I wanted to accomplish in life blossomed and grew and surrounded me as I continued to grow and develop during the crucial early years of childhood.

Her belief in me was so strong and was passed on to me so completely that it honestly never occurred to me to question whether I could accomplish something as a blind person. My only consideration was how I would accomplish that something. Since this attitude was passed on to my older brother and sisters and to all the children in the neighborhood, I spent my early years in what I later realized was an insular world of equal treatment and open acceptance.

It was a shock to me to later learn that I would be denied participation, or rejected out-of-hand, because of my blindness. I was outraged and looked to my mother to explain how people, adults and other children, could get away with such unfair, unfounded, and otherwise absolutely ludicrous treatment of me. She responded as usual with understanding and empathy, education about the reality of discrimination, and confirmation that the problem was not my blindness but the ignorance of others and, in her book, their unethical reaction to blindness. She insisted that I could rise above such ill treatment, find another way to accomplish my goals, and, perhaps, provide a little enlightenment in the process. Thus began my lifelong commitment to public education regarding disability and the seeds of activism that planted me firmly in the middle of the disability movement as an adult.

I can say, without any hint of equivocation, that I owe my independent spirit and my conviction that I have a right to that independence and to pursue the goals that I set for myself to that young woman who made it her business to be the best mother to me that she could be. She was and still is all that, and much more, to me. Though it was more than twenty-five years ago that she handed over—or I took—the reins of my own life (we're still arguing about that), she still provides me a willing ear, a little tea and sympathy, and a swift kick in the butt to get me moving toward finding a solution.

Nowadays, she shares her philosophy of disability (it would never occur to her to call it the "independent living philosophy") with her peers as they begin to encounter poorer vision, decreased mobility, shortness of breath, reduced stamina, and any of a number of things associated with advancing years. I know that she uses my life and my accomplishments as examples to follow, embellishing shamelessly and never pausing to give herself credit for being the impetus behind all that I do. The only time I ever hear her acknowledge her role is when we've been "discussing" something I plan to do, like my recent thousand-mile move from Mississippi to Virginia to pursue career advancement. She finally ends our discussion by saying, "I set out to make you independent, and damn if I didn't do a good job."

~

DONNA SMITH *is a training and technical assistance specialist for Easter Seals Project ACTION, a national program funded by the Federal Transit Administration to enhance transportation options for people with disabilities. She has worked for twenty-four years as a disability advocate and holds a B.A. in Psychology from Mississippi State University. She has been conducting training workshops and making public presentations on disability issues since 1985 and believes that communication is her greatest strength.*

Donna is dedicated to the disability movement and works— through both professional and personal efforts—to advocate for systems and attitudinal change. She believes strongly that every individual has the right to life, liberty, and the pursuit of happiness, and that this right should not be diminished by discriminatory actions based on disability or any other perceived differences. She has one daughter, age twenty-one, and currently lives in Arlington, Virginia.

CREATIVE PATHWAYS

Paul Kahn

I WISH MY PARENTS HAD KNOWN that I would grow up to have a satisfying life—a life enriched by independence, fulfilling work, a loving partner, and good friends.

I know my parents worried about me. When I was young there were no laws guaranteeing people with disabilities the right to equal education, community access, and protection against discrimination. My parents had to fight hard to instill in me the capacity to thrive. While much has improved, raising a child with a disability can still be difficult. Reflecting on my own childhood, I have some ideas to share.

I believe that human beings have two basic needs: the need to feel competent and independent and the need to belong and be cared about. Having a full life depends on satisfying these needs. But some children with disabilities have difficulty doing that. My physical weakness prevented me from achieving the milestones of independence that I saw other children celebrating—learning to walk, dress themselves, ride a bike, swing a baseball bat, and venture off on their own. I remained as dependent as an infant because I needed my parents to do almost everything for me, from dressing and toileting to cutting my food.

It was also difficult for me to feel that I belonged in the world. The physical environment excluded me with steps, curbs, and narrow doors, and I couldn't go to the inaccessible neighborhood schools, where most children find friends. When I was able to venture out with my parents' help, people treated me with rude stares or condescension. For me, the normal pathways to independence and belonging were blocked.

Parents can help by guiding their children toward alternative pathways. One most important way my parents guided me was encouraging my artistic creativity. I had a talent for the visual arts, which they nurtured by getting me art lessons, taking me to museums, buying me materials, and engaging in a variety of arts themselves. Drawing, painting, and sculpting gave me a sense of independence and competence because I could do them well and by myself. They also increased my sense of belonging. Through my artwork, I could communicate my feelings and, therefore, felt less alone. The admiration and praise I received from my parents and others made me more confident and outgoing. Sitting at our kitchen table with my paints, crayons, and clay, I felt that I was part of a world of artists where I was valued and accepted, unlike the playground world, where all that seemed to matter was how hard you could hit a ball or throw a punch.

The ability to create has continued to be an important part of my identity. A sense of identity is formed over time. It is a process of challenge and growth for all children, but children with disabilities often struggle harder.

The first stage of identity development is the recognition of being a separate individual. Children with disabilities can find this more difficult if they are overprotected and never cut the proverbial cord. Like me, some may be afraid to assert their individuality because they don't want to upset their parents. My brother, who had the same disability as I in an even more severe form, died when he was nine and I was six. As the survivor, I felt responsible for making up for my parents' loss by being very good and never complaining about the frustrations of being disabled. Denying my anger, I denied who I was.

Parents can help with this stage of identity development by being attentive, but not obsessed. When parents have their own interests and social lives, they and their children are both better off. When children are a parent's whole world, they find it harder to separate and become individuals. I remember hating when my parents left me with a sitter and went out to a movie or to visit friends. Now, I'm grateful that they had their lives and tried to let me have mine.

Parents can also help by being respectful of children's feelings. Looking back, I wish my parents had done a better job of helping me cope with my survivor's guilt. But, given their own profound grief, I can understand how overwhelming it might have been for them to pay attention to mine.

The second stage of identity development concerns the beginnings of initiative and independence. Children can have difficulty at this stage if they are unable to become more in control of their bodies, are too tightly supervised, and are not allowed take some risks.

Parents can help in two ways at this stage. First, encourage children to express preferences and make choices. A relatively minor choice, such as letting them decide what clothes they want to wear, can be important. If my mother had taken me shopping, I would have matured by having to practice making decisions and I would have felt that the way I dressed was an expression of my individuality and taste, not hers. Second, encourage children to take as much responsibility as possible. I can still remember the intense satisfaction I got when my father let me help him with household tasks such as painting the trim on the storm windows. If children are supposed to do certain therapies or take certain medications, let them start trying to remember these routines. In this way, they can develop pride and self-confidence, and, in the long run, they will be safer.

In the third stage, older children and adolescents must develop an optimistic sense of what their lives as adults will be like. Children with disabilities can have difficulty envisioning a good life if they don't see a way of becoming independent and don't feel attractive and able to form intimate relationships. When I became a young adult, because there were no personal care attendant programs, I had no idea how I would ever break my dependence on my parents. And, being acutely conscious of how different I was from the conventional standards of attractiveness, I had no sexual self-confidence.

Parents can help at this stage by connecting children with successful adult role models who can demonstrate the real possibilities for the future. Parents can also teach about human sexuality. Discussing this subject openly conveys the message that intimacy can and should be part of everyone's life.

This is also the time to begin making realistic plans for the future—when mom and dad won't be around anymore. If children can foresee how they will continue to thrive when that happens, they will face the future with more confidence. For my family, this meant finding a public school system that would accept and accommodate me and prepare me for college—and ultimately moving into the community.

As I reflect on my life, I want to emphasize—probably because it was difficult for me—the importance of expressing feelings, especially feelings of anger and loss. Sometimes, parents can feel guilty for giving birth to a child with a disability or "allowing" a disabling accident to happen. They feel helpless to ease their child's emotional pain. To avoid their own feelings of guilt and helplessness, they may stifle their child's expression of feelings.

But, experience has led me to appreciate uncomfortable feelings. They are signs of vitality that connect us to each other. Parents can best respond to a child's feelings by listening with empathy and respect. I strongly advise against saying things like: "Be a brave boy and don't cry" or "Other children are worse off than you." Such statements can make children feel humiliated and rejected. Parents also need to avoid unloading their own feelings on their children. As I did, children can feel responsible for making their parents happy and can feel frightened and guilty if they see their parents suffering.

Parents' feelings are important, too. From time to time, you will probably feel some sorrow and may ask: "Why me?" or "Can I cope with this?" But, at the same time, you will experience and relish the usual blessings of parenthood, and you may well discover within yourself personal strength and a capacity for growth that you never would have thought possible. For example, my parents became activists and spearheaded the passage of a state law that created the first of its kind day camp for children like me.

I am very proud of my parents. They weren't perfect, and neither is my life. Living with a severe disability remains a constant challenge that entails managing caregivers, maneuvering through service systems, and taking care of my health. I have been able to meet that challenge because my parents gave me their love and made me feel worthwhile. I strongly believe that the most important task of parenting is giving your children a foundation of self-respect. Everything else—your happiness and theirs—flows from that.

~

PAUL KAHN, M.ED., *has centronuclear myopathy. For more than twenty years, he has been a writer, editor, psychological counselor, and disability rights advocate. He has written or coauthored six books and published more than twenty articles in national publications. He is also a published poet and produced playwright. Among the awards he has received are a fellowship for residency at the Vermont Studio Center from the Christopher Reeve Paralysis Foundation, a professional development grant from the Massachusetts Cultural Council, a Newton (Massachusetts) Cultural Council Artist Grant, a Personal Achievement Award for Massachusetts from the Muscular Dystrophy Association, a Making a Difference Award from the Understanding Handicaps Program of Newton, and an Alumni Award for Outstanding Achievement in the Arts and Humanities from Boston University.*

Paul is married and lives with his wife, Ruth, in Newton, Massachusetts.

MY SECRET CHILDHOOD EXISTENCE

Taryn L. Hook

Dear Mom and Dad:
First, I want you to know that no child could ever have kinder or more loving parents. You both did everything in your power to make sure I felt safe and secure. You taught me to beware of strangers, to stay away from drugs, about sexually transmitted diseases, to respect myself, and, most of all, that I was loved. For these blessings, I am forever grateful.

However, Mom and Dad, there is one important item you missed. Don't be alarmed. As I grew up, no one in the adult world saw the signs. It is a taboo topic, a topic our culture often prefers to "sweep under the rug." I don't blame you. Without any training or knowledge yourself, how could you have seen it in me? This deadly intruder is mental illness. One in five of us will be affected by its catastrophic effects, yet few will obtain the treatment they so desperately need.

Let's review my life for just a bit. I'll let you in on my secret childhood existence; the hell that no one knew about—no one but the darkness and the demons that roamed my tortured child mind. I do this in the spirit of healing—with the hope that this examination will help other parents see the signs and symptoms that our family missed.

It all started when I was seven. Voices in my head screamed terrible expletives at Jesus Christ. The more I tried to stop them, the more prolific they became. I was terrified that God would take revenge on me, so I devised a plan to stave off God's wrath. I began arranging my stuffed animals in a certain way around my bed and around the perimeter of my room. Voices told me I had to make certain motions and retrace my steps in a specific way so that God would forgive me.

You didn't notice the strange formations of stuffed animals when you tucked me in. But if a medical professional had told you about the symptoms of a certain mental illness in as much detail as sexually transmitted diseases or drug abuse, you would have suspected that I had a condition called obsessive compulsive disorder (OCD).

The sufferers of OCD believe that unless they perform certain rituals, horrible things will happen to themselves, their family, or friends. As I grew older, my OCD blossomed. I did rituals of all sorts right in front of you, but you didn't see what you weren't looking for. My teachers didn't notice either. Even the school psychologist and counselor missed my rituals.

Some of my rituals included arranging and rearranging pencils, moving knickknacks around the house in different combinations, retracing my steps, counting things over and over, touching things repeatedly, and attempting to make items look symmetrical—such as aligning rows of peanuts or apples, for example. At the family dinner table, I touched the food on my plate with my fork in "just the right way" so the "vibes" would be positive and no one would get hurt. Then I would bring a glass of milk up to my mouth and put it down—bring it up again, put it down again. Over and over.

Eventually, the kids on the playground started to notice my strange behavior and made fun of me. The adult on duty at the playground didn't notice my distress and I had no words for what I was going through, so I took matters into my own hands. I vowed to do my rituals in secret. Thus, I started ritualizing in bathroom stalls. At home, I spent copious amounts of time in my room doing rituals to stave off demons that I thought were coming to annihilate our family.

I was always labeled the smart, precocious child that got straight As, so no one felt the need to check on me. They just assumed I was reading or studying. Mom and Dad and all the parents out there, this is one important thing I want to you to know. Academic success does not indicate that a child lacks mental problems. I am proof of that. In that room, that horrible room, I studied and earned good grades, but I also spent thousands of hours doing meaningless rituals and fearing the wrath of ghosts and demons. I believe I slept with my light on almost every night of my life.

Mom and Dad, if we had to do it all over again, I would suggest that you come into my room and play detective. Ask me blunt questions. What was I doing in my room all that time? Was everything all right? Why were the stuffed animals arranged in rows? Did I feel compelled by an outside force to put them there? Did I count things over and over in my head? Did I hear voices? You would have then assured me that anything I said—no matter how bizarre—would be taken seriously.

You certainly tried your best to ensure I was healthy. You faithfully took me to the doctor for my checkup every year, and not a single doctor detected anything wrong or asked me any questions about my mental health.

As awful as OCD was, it wasn't the only mental illness troubling me. Do you remember when I used to wake up screaming? Do you recall that I would become hysterical—on airplanes and roller coasters, in cars and high places, and, sometimes spontaneously, without any discernible stimulus?

Remember when I was twelve? I woke up frantic and terrified, running around the house screaming until dawn. You took exactly the right steps. You made an appointment with one of the finest specialists in northern California the very next day. The doctor declared me healthy and insinuated that I was simply a "histrionic" child who wanted attention. I would grow out of this phase, he said. If not, there was a rare medical condition that might explain my outbursts, he maintained. I know you wanted to believe the doctor, since he was from one of the best universities in the world—yet your instincts told you something different. I know how confusing it must have been for you.

Your instincts were right. I suffered from severe chronic panic disorder. The symptoms include a choking feeling; tunnel vision; a feeling of depersonalization (the feeling of split consciousness—remember all that gibberish I yelled about the earth spinning—I didn't articulate it well, but I felt like there were two of me spinning in outer space); severe agitation; and white, clammy hands and face.

The moral: no matter how famous or renowned a doctor may be, you know your child better than anyone. If the doctor tells you something you intuitively know is wrong, get more opinions until you feel comfortable

Eventually, as an adult, I was hospitalized three times. I don't blame my childhood. I lay the blame squarely on the stigma of mental illness. We are taught to look for signs of drug abuse or cancer, but as a culture we aren't taught the signs of depression or other mental illness. Fortunately, the tides are changing with greater media coverage of mental health issues and parity laws that offer equal insurance coverage for mental health issues.

Mom and Dad, I know you feel guilty for not detecting my mental illness when I was a child. But you couldn't have known. No one knew. If the best doctors didn't know, how could you? And besides, everything turned out all right. I am fine now. I have the best mental health care available. I have a wonderful new life. You have given me the most amazing support since I have been diagnosed. Our experiences can help countless other parents. There is nothing to feel unhappy about. There is only light, hope, and the happiness of a new day.

With the greatest love and admiration,
Your Daughter

TARYN HOOK *is a lawyer, mental health advocate, and writer living in northern California. Her work has appeared in a variety of publications, including the* Santa Clara Law Review, Occupational Therapy Week, UC Davis Magazine, Hadrasaur Tales, Horrorfind, Reptiles *magazine, and* Fairbanks Daily News-Miner. *Throughout most of her life, she zealously hid her mental illness for fear of being labeled "crazy." In her early thirties, however, her mental state rapidly deteriorated and she was hospitalized. In the hospital, she realized that individuals with mental illness were normal people from all walks of life. Afterward, she no longer feared revealing her mental illness. She gained a new mission in life: to tear down the stigma and misconceptions about mental illness. Several years ago, she was featured on a Discovery Channel special about OCD. Today, she works for a mental health agency that helps people with mental illness find employment.*

ANOTHER WAY OF SEEING

Deborah Kent

RECENTLY, I READ that our first memories contain themes that remain crucial throughout our lives. When I think back, I find that most of my earliest memories have to do with touch. For me as a blind child, touch meant seeing—seeing in the widest sense, seeing as perceiving and understanding. When I was allowed to touch things, I was in my glory. When I heard the dreaded words, "Don't touch!" I felt excluded, shut away from knowledge and experience.

The first scene that comes to mind occurred when I was about twenty months old. My father is lifting me in his arms so I can reach over the edge of a large cardboard box. Inside the box, my hands discover a pile of warm, wriggling bodies—soft fur, bony heads, wet noses, and curious, lapping tongues. "See?" Dad says. "Fluffy's puppies! Look!"

In another memory, I am perched on a stool at the kitchen counter while my mother prepares a chicken dinner. Patiently, she shows me the cold, plucked bird before us. She points out the legs, the wings, the breast, and the place where the head used to be. My hands explore every nuance of poultry anatomy.

In a somewhat later memory, my cousin holds a crayfish captive in a jar. I beg to touch it, but the grown-ups say no. They insist that its claws will pinch my fingers. Someone gives me a stick and says I can touch the crayfish with that. But I can't learn anything about this mysterious creature by probing it with the tip of a stick. I need to study it with my hands, and when I am not allowed, I burst into tears of frustration.

Sighted children look at everything around them, gathering volumes of information through their eyes. The figurines on a shelf, the umbrella leaning in the corner, the heavy drapes that might provide a place for hide-and-seek—each new object is a source of fascination. To my immense good fortune, my parents instinctively recognized that, though I could not see with my eyes, I had the same need as any other child to learn about and enjoy my surroundings. My parents understood that my blindness need not hold me back. My experience of the world could be rich and meaningful through the sense of touch.

Somehow my parents realized that I needed plenty of hands-on experience with the everyday objects sighted children take in almost automatically by eye. When I was a toddler, my mother made time in her hectic schedule to take me on a walk nearly every afternoon. She showed me split-rail fences, mailboxes, fire hydrants, lawn statues, birdbaths, and telephone poles. We sat on the ground so I could examine dead leaves, dandelions, and acorns. Mom even showed me sidewalks, manhole covers, and curbstones. Nothing was too ordinary for our attention. Everything was worth inspecting.

Expeditions with my father tended to be more adventurous. Sometimes he took me on walks in the woods, where we crashed through the underbrush and got our shoes caked with mud. On other days, we explored the construction sites in our suburban development. In half-finished houses, I learned that doors and windows fit into frames and discovered that bathroom pipes descend through holes in the flooring.

My parents had the wisdom to know that for me, as for all children, examining an object once was not enough. Sighted children have unending opportunities to look at trees and fences and bicycles. I, too, needed to reinforce my perception of everyday things by touching them again and again. The inventiveness and unflagging patience of my parents enabled me to create a vast library of tactile images, a mental storehouse of information that has expanded throughout my lifetime. Furthermore, my parents' encouragement nourished my natural curiosity. I grew up hungering for firsthand knowledge of the world. I wanted a hands-on view of my cousin's crayfish and wouldn't settle for less.

Sight and touch are both spatial senses, conveying information about the shape, size, and placement of objects. While sight can be effective at long distances, touch is "up close and personal." For this reason, in our society at least, touch is often suspect. After all, if someone touches an object, it may get broken or even stolen. "Hands off!" children are warned from an early age. They absorb the message that touch is forbidden and may carry a penalty.

As the sighted parent of a blind child, you may find it hard to accept that touch is a valid and necessary mode of seeing. You may have to recognize and set aside your own discomfort with touch before you can give your child the freedom she needs. People will stare at her exploring hands. Some may frown with disapproval, and you will have to explain that your child is looking with her hands because she is blind. But blindness is not shameful. It is simply a different way of being in the world.

By helping your child explore and learn in her own way, you will give her a lifelong gift. She will share in the pool of knowledge that is basic to her peers. She will be better equipped to take part in their games, to understand their humor, to join in their mischief, and to dream up pranks of her own. She will be part of the world around her, and she will know that she belongs.

As your child grows up, he will become your teacher as much as you will be his. He will show you that he can accomplish most tasks without sight, by relying on touch, hearing, and common sense. He will read Braille instead of print and will explore the neighborhood using a long white cane. Rarely will blindness stop him from doing the things he wants to do—though the anxieties of other people will sometimes stand in his way. When he wants to try something new, even if you think it will be hard, help him think of ways and means.

Have faith in his abilities, and he will learn to have faith in himself. Living in a world where most people are sighted, your child will need contact with other people who are blind. Blind adults who are working and raising families can be invaluable role models for your child, and they can answer many key questions you have as a parent. From the beginning, it will be important for you to seek out blind teens and adults. Get to know them, and learn about their lives. Make them a part of your child's life and your own.

By helping your child reach out to the world, you will unlock her fullest potential. She will have a chance to make unique contributions to her family, school, and community. Her blindness will always be a difference, but it need never be a tragedy.

~

DEBORAH KENT *was born in Glen Ridge, New Jersey, and grew up in nearby Little Falls. She studied at special Braille classes and then became the first totally blind student to attend the local public high school. She graduated from Oberlin College and received a master's degree from Smith College School for Social Work. For four years, she was a social worker at University Settlement House on New York's Lower East Side.*

In 1975, Deborah moved to San Miguel de Allende, Mexico, where she wrote her first young adult novel, Belonging *(People with Disabilities Press, 2002). The book draws upon her experiences attending public school for the first time. Also in San Miguel, she helped to found the Centro de Crecimiento, a school for children with disabilities.*

Deborah is the author of numerous young adult novels and nonfiction titles for children. She now lives in Chicago with her husband, children's author R. Conrad Stein, and their daughter, Janna.

AS NORMAL AS CAN BE

Juan B. K. Magdaraog

G ROWING UP WITH A DISABILITY is not easy. For more than fifteen of my twenty-six years, I've had to cope up with a disability. Although it hasn't been easy, I've managed to keep a good,
positive attitude throughout all these years. There have been times
when I've thought of giving up—telling myself that life is just too
hard and asking myself, "What's the use of it all?" Thank God, my
parents brought me up the way they did. Had they not, I would have
given in to negative feelings and self-pity.

The first ten years of my life seemed normal. I was physically a
little bit weaker than other kids, but my disability wasn't very evident until I reached the age of ten. My parents brought me to several doctors. At first I was diagnosed as having muscular dystrophy.
Only a few years ago, we discovered that I actually had acid maltase
deficiency, also known as Pompe disease, a progressive neuromuscular disease.

When my parents found out I had a disability, their world was
shattered. How can their firstborn have a disability? The questions
came flowing into their minds—all the how, why, where, and when
questions. After some time, when the initial shock was over, my parents made a decision. It was to be the most important decision that
they would make concerning my life. They decided to raise me as a
normal kid—no matter what. While they might give me certain

allowances, they would not treat me any differently from their other son. I would have the same privileges and responsibilities as any child of my age.

I learned a great deal from my parents. One of the most important lessons was that although I might be different, that doesn't mean I'm a lesser person than other people. They also taught me to work hard and not give up. If I can't be strong physically, I can still be strong mentally. They also taught me: "Don't ever let anyone tell you that they're better than you. You can do other things that they can't. Think positive. It's useless to dwell upon things that never were or never will be. As long as you're alive, there's hope. Miracles do happen." And, most important of all, "Anything is possible with God by your side—keep the faith."

As the years went by and my disability progressed, life became more difficult. The gravity of my disability rose and my independence fell. Growing up in a third-world country has meant that access to health care and disability resources are not as great as in developed nations. While my family was middle class by my country's standards, health care was expensive. My dad had to buy a wheelchair abroad because he wanted me to have a decent one—a chair that I'd be happy with and comfortable using.

Despite the high cost of health care and the lack of awareness about the needs of people with disabilities, I had one thing going for me. Labor wasn't expensive in our country. My family was able to hire a caregiver for me as well as a driver to help me get around. This has been a great help for me, both physically and mentally. The caregiver was able to do the things that adaptive devices might do for a person with a disability, while the driver gave me freedom to explore the world around me.

Since hiring a caregiver in developed countries is expensive, people with disabilities may have one of their family members take care of them. While this might be good for some people and situations, this might not always be so. Why? Personally, I think that the relationship between family members might be strained because some members might feel that an unusual burden has been placed upon them. Feelings of resentment might surface between the person with a disability and the family members. In addition, having someone, independent of your family, involved in the care of the person with a disability as a job brings about a sense of detachment. The relationship is professional. The caregiver is there to provide a service; you are providing him with a livelihood.

Having a caregiver also gives the person with a disability a sense of independence as well as a life away from his or her family. Because my relationship with my caregiver has been a professional one, I did not have to worry about whether or not he was obliged to be there. Instead, I was able to concentrate on growing up and living. Fostering a positive relationship with your family is fine, but fostering an independent relationship with yourself, away from the family, is also important.

By hiring someone to be my caregiver, my parents helped me become who I am today. I feel normal and have a sense of identity because of it. I see myself as an independent individual. I don't have to rely on a family member to care for me. While they are ready to care for me, they chose to hire someone while they can afford it. They know that a life away from them is also important—not just for me, but also for my parents and sibling. They are not pressured into revolving their lives around me. My brother has the freedom to do as any young person does. To give him credit, he has been there for me whenever I needed him.

As a result of my parents' thoughtfulness and generosity, I've managed to live a somewhat normal life. Finishing college, looking for and finding a job, and having good relationships with friends, as well as a relationship with a special someone are all things that so-called normal people do. I attribute this full life to all that my parents have done for me.

In my opinion, one of the most overlooked aspects of bringing up a person with a disability is paying attention to that person's emotional needs. Parents with children with disabilities can overlook the fact that there is an emotional price that can come with having a disability. For me, it is often the emotional problems that are more complex and harder to get past than the physical problems.

In every respect, people with physical disabilities are the same as normal people. They have the same wants, needs, desires, and so on. Yet, due to an individual's physical disabilities, frustrations may arise that might lead to emotional difficulties. I'm grateful because my parents addressed these issues as well. The help they gave me by instilling the values that they taught me and their choice of having a caregiver look after me gave me a chance to live a normal life.

Whenever certain issues or problems arose, I have been able to deal with them independently. If I needed help, I was able to go to my parents. By having a separate life away from my parents, I have had the chance to grow up as a person.

Looking back, I do wish that my parents talked to me more about sex. Let's face it, sex will always be an issue, whether you have a disability or not. A better understanding of sex and how it impacts your life is helpful. Especially when a person's disability is severe, an open discussion on how to handle sexual relationships, and all the related issues that come with such relationships, is needed. Talking about such issues can help the person with a disability cope as such topics come up.

While there are things that I wish might have been different, my parents have done enough. They have cared for me, instilled in me the attitudes that have guided me through all these years, and provided me with the means to attain a sense of normalcy in my life. They have brought me up to be as close to normal as possible despite the circumstances. My family has sacrificed a lot for me. I am very thankful.

~

BORN AND RAISED *in Manila, Philippines, Juan Magdaraog has acid maltase deficiency, a slow, progressive neuromuscular disease. Despite the physical challenges, Juan managed to attend school and graduate with a B.S. in Industrial Design from one of the leading universities in the Philippines. Juan worked for almost two years with a talent management company in its Web/technical department before rejoining his cousin in a small multimedia development company they put up years ago.*

Juan enjoys watching movies, surfing the Internet, and going out with friends. He is active in Singles for Christ (SFC), a Christian community for single people. Through SFC, Juan had the privilege of sharing his life story and speaking in front of thousands of members about how someone with a disability can still be a productive member of society.

IF MOM ONLY KNEW

Darren R. Cecil

THE MAN STOOD OUTSIDE a five-and-dime store grasping a cup of pencils in his only hand. The pencils were his livelihood. A modern peddler, he humbly displayed his wares. The mother vowed that this would not be the life of her son.

The mother knew that something was awry. She was hospitalized for blood clots. She feared for the health of the baby. God told her that the child would be missing something.

She was fiercely determined to make her son self-sufficient. She taught him to dress himself, eat his own meals, and do everything that most kids his age could do with the exception of one thing—the mother still regrets that she could never teach her child how to tie his shoes.

If only the mother knew back then that her son would own his own business and possess a master's degree. She would have worried less about her son's job prospects. If she only knew. . . .

The boy began to realize he looked different than the other kids; he was born with one arm missing below the elbow. Mother told him that God didn't have enough arms up in heaven. For two years, the boy thought that God had a machine and He was short of arms. Until one day, the boy went to a classmate's birthday party. The classmate was born just a few days after him. The friend had two arms.

The boy came to his mother with sadness and shock. "Why does he have an arm and I don't?" pleaded the boy. "He was born after me, and God gave him an arm. Will I ever grow a hand?"

Fighting back the tears, the mother replied truthfully, and then firmly told him, "You were born this way. People will laugh at you. They will stare. They may fear you. You are to come to me if they mistreat you. Your hook is just as good as a hand. Now live your life the very best you can."

If she only knew back then how her child's hurts taught him compassion for all people. She would marvel how his own discomforts taught him to comfort others. If she'd only known how her strong words, positive attitude, and honesty would shape the boy's determination. If she only knew. . . .

From the time the boy was three months old, and all through college, the boy was a patient at a renowned teaching hospital. In a large, cold amphitheater full of doctors and medical students, the boy removed his shirt. The boy sat upon a gurney. The physicians discussed the disability of the child as if the child was not present in the room. The doctors stared at the boy, took notes, and inquired about the disability. The chief doctor painfully grabbed the boy's arm and bent it back, forward, and side-to-side. The interrogation, at first, was extremely intimidating and overwhelmingly frightening for the boy.

The mother tried to normalize the grueling experience. After visiting the hospital, she took him to breakfast and then to a drugstore to purchase Tic Tacs. Next, they either went shopping at a Filene's Basement "Darwinian Dollar Days" sale or took a tour of Boston's rich historical and cultural sites. Then it was time for lunch. Typically, the two grabbed a sandwich; the restaurant had a giant teapot hanging over the entrance with actual steam pouring out of the pot. After lunch, they rode the bus and talked during the long walk home from their stop. The mother made the day seem like an adventure so that the boy didn't feel like just a guinea pig.

Over time, the child became comfortable with the doctors. He began to make jokes and challenge the doctors' comments. If the mother only knew that being poked, prodded, and treated as a specimen to be studied would prepare her child to address large audiences with ease. If she only knew. . . .

When he was six or seven years old, the physicians asked the boy to share his adjustment to a lifelong disability with adults who had recently become disabled—mostly Vietnam veterans. The boy was frightened, but he never hesitated to share how much fun he had and how he could do almost everything anyone else could do. The recent amputees were usually gracious and polite to the young boy. The boy learned at an early age how to educate and motivate.

Teaching veterans would one day inspire the boy to teach college students and companies. A boy who once motivated demoralized men now motivates many others. If his mother only knew. . . .

The boy also loved to play, and he gained peer acceptance by succeeding in sports. As a sophomore in high school, he tried out for the junior varsity basketball team. The coach cut him.

The boy worked hard on his game throughout the year. In the winter, he shoveled off the basketball courts so he could shoot baskets.

The tryouts came around again, and he played extremely well. The day the team roster was posted, he excitedly walked toward the coach's office to see his name. When he walked by, other players became eerily silent. One said, "Sorry, man, I can't believe you didn't make it." Dumbfounded, the boy saw that his name was omitted from the roster.

The boy sprinted to find the varsity coach. Unable to control his composure, the boy told the coach that in previous conversations the coach stated how the boy could improve his game. The player had done all that was asked.

The coach acknowledged the boy's improvement. But he explained that the boy was cut because he could not dribble with his left hand. The boy's mouth dropped. The coach must be joking. When the boy realized the coach was serious, the boy began to laugh. It did not matter to the coach that the player was considered the second-best player who tried out.

The boy became extremely focused and polite. He asked the coach to evaluate performance on what the boy could do on the court. He told the coach that he wanted to be reinstated on the team for a two-week probationary period. After the two-week "tryout," the junior varsity coach and the varsity coach could evaluate the boy's skills. If the skills were not acceptable, they could make a decision to cut the boy—and he would never try out again. The coach acquiesced. The player never revealed to his parents what had taken place.

The boy not only passed the probationary period but also became the second-best scorer on the team. At the end-of-the-year banquet, the coach shared the story with the attendees. He said that as a teacher, he was taught a lesson on determination and prejudice by a player who couldn't dribble with his left hand.

His mother said, "Why didn't you tell us?"

The boy said, "You told me sometimes I had to stick up for myself. I thought this was the time."

Today, the boy is a man, dedicated to sticking up for people with disabilities. He owns his own business. He lives in a nice home, is happily married, and has three beautiful children. He went on to play sports in college. He has received numerous awards and innumerable blessings and gifts from God. He has accomplished so much—although he still can't dribble with his left hand or tie his shoes.

Perhaps if the mother had known then of her son's life purpose, she would have felt a deeper peace. The ties that bind and being able to tie one's life together are far more important than shoe ties that keep a child from tripping. Her boy may have fallen, but he always landed on his feet. If his mother had only known. . . .

~

DARREN CECIL *was born with one arm missing below the elbow. He was diagnosed with an eye disease while attending college, which resulted in a cornea transplant.*

He served as a poster child for both Easter Seals and the March of Dimes. He established the Darren Cecil Scholarship for people with disabilities at Emerson College.

An international lecturer on disability issues, Darren is the owner of DisABILITY Resources Consulting (DRC). He fosters awareness and enhances sensitivity to the needs of customers and employees with disabilities. He shares his personal experiences with a disability to foster an inclusive, comfortable learning environment. DRC's client list includes Fortune 500 corporations; professional sports teams; international associations; federal, state, and municipal governments; not-for-profit organizations; and universities and colleges.

Darren is also the author of The Disability Handbook: Because, from Time to Time, Everyone Needs a Helping Hand *(DisABILITY Resources Consulting, 2001).*

3

PARENTAL
EXPECTATIONS

AFFIRMATION AND CHALLENGE

Lucy C. Spruill

O N A SUNNY AFTERNOON in 1968, I went to my class at the School of Social Work, wheeling in breathlessly a few minutes late, as usual. Mr. Parsons, the young professor, was not at the front of the room lecturing. Instead, my classmates were standing in clumps of four or five, talking in hushed tones. I joined one of the clumps and soon learned that Mrs. Parsons had just delivered a baby boy with spina bifida and the baby was in intensive care. My fellow students were whispering about what a terrible tragedy this was and that the baby would probably die—which would be a "blessing."

My heart went out to this young couple, as my husband and I were expecting our first baby in about a month and I had lived a happy and satisfying life for all of twenty-three years after being born with spina bifida. I was concerned that Mr. Parsons and his wife have a chance to hear messages that would offset the "gloom-and-doom" reactions I had heard in class that day.

I was a typically self-conscious, young adult woman, newly married, pregnant with my first child, still in graduate school, and with not much "real-life" experience under my belt. I was especially self-conscious when talking about myself, usually just murmuring a few words about a "problem with my back" when anyone asked the inevitable "What happened to you?" about the wheelchair I use. On this day, I realized that my experiences might help someone else and made an appointment with Mr. Parsons.

I told Mr. Parsons that I had been born with spina bifida and shared as many details as I could about the things I enjoyed as a child and young adult. I expressed hope that his baby would survive and live a long and happy life, and I answered his questions about what this baby's needs would be as best I could. Eagerly absorbing as much as I could tell him, he said that, for the first time since the baby was born, he could form pictures of his role as a parent and his little boy's life. As an expectant father, he had pictures in his mind of playing football with his son and being a Scout leader. But, all the pictures had disappeared and he had nothing to replace them with—until our talk gave him new visions. Mr. Parsons and I laughed and cried a lot together during that conversation.

Our talk gave me new insight about why it is important to have adults with disabilities participating actively in every community, to serve as role models for children with disabilities and their families. It also gave me a compelling reason to overcome my reluctance to talk about my own experiences.

When I obtained my birth certificate to apply for a passport, I pictured my own mother and father (now deceased) as new parents. I realized how young and far from home they were when I, their first child, was born. It was during the closing days of World War II. Almost nothing was known about medical treatment and special education for children with disabilities. Like the Parsons, my parents were bombarded with "gloom-and-doom" reactions from friends and medical professionals, who gave them the usual "best advice" of those days—to place this infant in an institution where she would get humane care for the few years she was likely to live, go on with their lives, and have other, healthy children.

Like most young people, it was many years before I appreciated the remarkable job my parents had done with the difficult task of nurturing, guiding, and stimulating me in the largely unsupportive social environment of the 1940s and 1950s. Trusting the values they had from their faith, family, and community, they decided to take me home and raise me as they would any other child, never wavering in the strength of that initial commitment.

Because my mother was initially depressed and overwhelmed following my birth, my father made the wise decision to move his vulnerable young family from the large city where they had gone to find work in the wartime economy to a rural Pennsylvania village where my mother could have the support of her parents and extended family. I grew up as the first grandchild in my mother's loving, extended family of Catholic immigrant coal miners and farmers. These working-class people had survived the Depression and a world war and understood that life often includes some hard times. In this culture, community, interdependence, and cooperation were valued rather than independence and competitiveness. Needing help was not seen as a problem—as long as one was also willing to give help when it was needed. They did not see the birth of a child with a disability as a tragedy and discouraged any inclination to self-pity that I or my parents may have had.

My parents respected health care professionals greatly and followed their instructions faithfully. But, they balanced that respect with trust in their instinctive inclination to adopt a hopeful "wait-and-see" attitude about the negative predictions for me of a short, miserable life followed by an early death. Each week, as we drove long distances to the city for my therapy and medical appointments, they never focused on the idea of a "cure." Their attitude helped me feel that while I should work to achieve the best functioning possible, I was perfectly OK just the way I was. This was just one of many subtle but important distinctions my parents helped me understand.

My mother and grandmother were my first "early intervention specialists," teaching me to read, write, and do simple arithmetic before I reached school age. They also dressed me in pretty clothes, curled my hair like Shirley Temple's, and told me that I was pretty.

And, I was included in the rich cultural life of the community. My favorite family picture shows my father whirling me around a dance floor to a polka at a community wedding when I was just a toddler.

When it came time for me to go to school, my parents fought successfully for homebound instruction when the district school board tried to refuse any education at all for me. This was a powerful early lesson in the importance of advocacy and further evidence of my parents' faith in my abilities and value as a person.

My mother realized that the five hours a week of homebound instruction I was provided was not a complete education. She and my grandmother encouraged me to enjoy educational television programs; provided me with good books; and taught me typing, shorthand, needlework, and Italian, which was their first language. Throughout my school years, my parents helped me discover and develop the abilities I had, rather than being concerned with those things I couldn't do. In keeping with the important values of our culture, they expected me to get good grades and grow up to work and contribute to the community.

As it turned out, I was the oldest of five children and was expected to do chores, help prepare meals, and take care of my younger brothers—just like my girlfriends in their families. I laugh when I remember one afternoon when my mother was trying to cook dinner, comfort a crying baby, and do the family ironing. My grandmother seized the ironing board; brought it to where I was sitting; and informed me that I needed to learn how to cook, clean, and do laundry—if I was going to amount to anything!

These developmental experiences were valuable in helping me acquire an image of myself as a competent and important member of my family and community. As I was growing up, messages from my family were much more powerful in shaping the person I was to become than the negative, limiting messages from movies and telethons; being excluded from school; and the dire predictions by professionals of a useless life and an early death. My family's positive messages helped me acquire the self-confidence I needed to begin

homemaking and child-rearing as a young woman—and to find raising my own family very satisfying and enjoyable.

My parents were not perfect. They were extremely authoritar-
ian, which generated commensurate rebelliousness in my brothers
and me, especially as we became young adults in the 1960s. As most
parents of children with disabilities, they were much more protective of me than my friends' parents were of them, and, once I left
home, I had a lot of catching up to do in social skills. But the foundation they gave me in the value of commitment to self, family, and
community far outweighed the limitations that were so typical of
the times in which they lived.

≈

LUCY SPRUILL *has been employed as a program director for United
Cerebral Palsy of Pittsburgh, Pennsylvania, since June 1998. Prior to
assuming this position, after a twenty-year career in maternal and
child health, she served as Americans with Disabilities Act coordinator for the city of Pittsburgh. She is also an instructor in the Schools
of Health and Rehabilitation Sciences and Social Work at the University of Pittsburgh. Lucy has received national recognition for advocacy, consultation, and training in the field of meaningful inclusion
and participation in community life for people with disabilities, particularly in the fields of health care and public transportation. She is
the mother of an adult son and daughter and a lifelong resident of
southwestern Pennsylvania.*

A STUBBORN SENSE OF ENTITLEMENT

Mike Ervin

THE CHILDHOOD IMAGE that endures in my mind is of my mother maneuvering two kids in wheelchairs down a bumpy sidewalk. She pushes my sister in front of her, steering with one hand, while she reaches back with the other hand and grabs my armrest, pulling me along behind. It's quite a contortion sometimes. She's practically walking sideways.

We arrive at the rusty station wagon. My mother lifts Chris, my sister (I call her Tina), into the front seat and me into the back. She flings the chairs into the tailgate area. Off we go.

My parents separated when I was ten and Tina was twelve, and my dad rarely came around again. He was never around much before that anyway. My mother was articulate and intelligent, but she was a high school dropout. She worked as a waitress at the time. Sometimes money was so tight she borrowed from our piggy banks. But she always put it back. I never noticed. I never felt poor. We lived in a brick house with a square lawn on a wide, clean city street. The refrigerator was always full.

With two kids in wheelchairs in perpetual tow, my mother looked like some sort of Catholic saint to some passersby. She would find that laughable. Saints are insufferably selfless martyrs who sacrifice their personal happiness for the benefit of others. But for her, being out and about with her kids was the pursuit of happiness. We were just going from point A to point B like everyone else.

My sister and I were raised with the expectation that because we were bright kids we could achieve greatness. Our job was to do well in school, go to college, find a profession we enjoyed, and be important contributors. But it wasn't because my mother had an activist agenda. She wasn't determined that we were going to show the world that kids with disabilities could do great things too. My mother set high standards for us because that's what mothers do. They're supposed to push their kids to achieve greatness. Why should we be any different?

My mother's best parental asset was her naiveté. It was quite radical in the 1960s for a single mom of two kids with muscular dystrophy to teach them to expect a lot out of themselves and out of life. But it just never occurred to her that because of our disabilities she should do it any other way.

My sister spent a month of her childhood in the hospital lying mostly on her back with full-length casts on her legs. A doctor convinced my mother that this was a necessary treatment to keep her knees from contracting.

Doctors prescribed a lot of braces for me. When I wore them all, it felt like a suit of armor: my leg braces—metal bars running up the inside and outside of both legs, leather straps around the shins, knees and thighs; my Milwaukee spinal brace—a leather corset with a hinged metal pelvic belt; a vertical metal bar running the length of my trunk in front and two more running up the back providing the skeletal structure; and, a padded chin rest. I moved as stiffly as Frankenstein when I wore my suit of armor.

The doctors told my mother that the Milwaukee brace would "suspend my spine" thus combating scoliosis. I was to wear it twenty-three hours a day forever, only taking it off to bathe. I pleaded and protested hard against the idea of spending all day and even sleeping in that awkward thing. My mother never put up much resistance. She only made me wear it during school hours.

The doctors wanted to surgically implant steel rods in my sister's back to secure her spine, which would have meant about a year of recovery time. The leg casting had been such a miserable episode that Tina bitterly opposed the surgery. My mother told the doctors no.

My mother never seemed convinced in her heart that these medical interventions were worth the discomfort they put us through. That's why she never pushed them on us much. It seemed to go against her instinct that our disabilities shouldn't keep us out of life. Time spent being medically compliant, unless really necessary, was better spent learning, playing, exploring—being a kid.

Soon after the casts were removed, my sister's legs both contracted anyway. I shed all my braces by the time I graduated from high school. My sister and I are both pushing fifty and are still doing fine with our contractions and scoliosis and all. That's a better case scenario than the doctors presented even if we had had heavy-duty medical interventions. My mother was right. We were better off spending that time in the sandbox.

When my sister was ready to start high school in 1968, my mother went to see the principals of the local Catholic and public schools. She wanted them to accept Tina as a student, but they turned her down flat. Something might happen and Tina could get hurt, they said. She might indeed get hurt, my mother said. Kids get hurt in school every day. And when they do, we patch them up and send them back into the ring.

But there were no education rights laws back then for kids with disabilities. If any principal didn't want us, they didn't have to take us. No questions asked.

So we went from our disability segregated public elementary school to an even more segregated state-run, kindergarten through high school, boarding school called the Illinois Children's Hospital School (ICHS).

Like many state institutions, it was Death Valley. Many of the kids were wards of the state dumped by their families. The quality of education was abysmal. There was no science class more complex than biology, no math class more complex than geometry. There were twenty-year-old kids in sixth grade. When these kids reached age twenty-one and had to leave, they'd probably go to a nursing home. If they didn't have to leave at twenty-one, they'd probably stay at ICHS forever.

My mother wanted us to be in a college prep program, but this was the best option she had because we were in wheelchairs. Few kids went on to college from ICHS. Few even got their diplomas. It was a holding cell for those who had been written off.

The walls were painted bright colors but the institutional pall was still heavy to me. Some kids had lived there since they were four years old. It made me cringe inside to wonder what would have happened to Tina and I had we come there that young. Our survival advantage was in the stubborn sense of entitlement my mother had given us. Without it, we might have come to believe, like the most lethargic among us, that we could only handle life in the tiniest of rationed doses and that aspirations are false hope.

We had no choice but to be there. We did our time, got our diplomas, and went on to college.

My mother winged it. There were no navigational guides for a single working mom raising two kids in wheelchairs. I'm glad there weren't because they may well have counseled her to play it safe and think small. They may even have presented a merciful rationale for abandoning us. Mother could never think of such things on her own.

In this undocumented frontier, she could have easily made many wrong turns but she generally avoided them by relying on her instinct to let kids seek out what excites them and makes them happy. We didn't have the time or desire as kids to mourn our disabilities. There was too much fun to be had. Kids have a strong natural sense of adventure. That's the joy of childhood. I'm ever grateful that my mother never saw disability as a reason to take that away from us.

~

MIKE ERVIN *is a journalist, playwright, radio producer, and disability rights activist living in Chicago. His play "The History of Bowling" and his other theater works have been produced across America.*

Among his published fiction is the short story, "Coitus Interruptus," in Staring Back, an Anthology of Writers with Disabilities *(Plum, 1997). By day, he is a freelance journalist and has published more than one thousand articles and essays—mostly on disability topics and jazz—in more than forty newspapers and magazines. He is also producer of "On a Roll," a nationally syndicated radio talk show on disability.*

As a longtime member of the direct action disability rights group ADAPT, Mike is proud to have been arrested more than a dozen times for civil disobedience.

INDEPENDENCE: LESSONS FROM MY MOM

Tameeka L. Hunter

I WOULD LIKE TO SHARE some of the lessons my mother taught me while I was growing up with a congenital disability. I believe that the lessons I have learned could be helpful to parents of other children with disabilities.

The most important lesson I learned is to try to be independent. When my mother and I would go out running errands and I would come across an architectural barrier, I would say, "Mama, help me to get up these stairs." She would say, "What would you do if I wasn't here?" I would give her a perplexed look and say, "But you are here." Then she would reply, "Pretend that I'm not here. What would you do to get up these steps?" This made me determined to do it on my own. I would figure out a way to do it myself. I would then look back at her triumphantly—I thought I had shown her—but she was never disappointed. Instead, she was always smiling back at me. At the time, I did not realize that she was trying to teach me to be independent.

Attitudinal and architectural barriers can threaten the independence of individuals with disabilities. People with disabilities cannot always be completely independent, but I think it is important for parents to teach their children to be as independent as they can. Attitudinal barriers cause all other barriers. For example, people would often stare at me. When this would happen, my mother would say, "If someone stares at you, stare right back, and then say hello." This was her way of teaching me not to let people objectify me. By staring back, it reminds people how uncomfortable it feels; by saying hello, it reminds them that I'm human.

Another lesson my mother taught me is that people are not always kind or sensitive. One day, while grocery shopping, I noticed a little girl about three years old looking at me as she tagged along with her mother. Eventually, her mother noticed that she was looking at me because she was probably curious about my crutches or how I walk. She quickly pulled her daughter away by the arm and curtly said, "Stop looking at her," with no further explanation. I wish she had taken the time to explain that although I have a disability and may do things differently than other people, I am a person, too. I believe the way the mother reacted taught her daughter to be fearful of people who look different from her, people with disabilities. In addition, her actions inadvertently conveyed that people with disabilities should be ignored and overlooked. Parents should encourage their children to ask questions and to learn about different people, including those with disabilities.

My mother taught me to be fearless, to never settle, and, ultimately, that disability is not an excuse for not trying. One example of this was when I was five years old and my school took a field trip to an ice skating rink. My teachers told me, as kindly as they could, that I would not be able to participate in this activity because I used crutches. At first this saddened me. Then I thought about some of the things that my mother had taught me. While the other students were skating, I went over to the equipment rental booth, grabbed a pair of skates in my size, and quickly put them on. I went out on the ice, crutches and all, and proceeded to skate for a few seconds. The photographer covering the field trip took a picture of me on the ice with my crutches. The headline read, "She Did It." After that, my teachers said, "We won't ever tell you that you can't do something again. From now on, we'll let you tell us."

My mother taught me to be realistic about my limitations, but to determine those limitations for myself. She also taught me not to allow people to tell me what I can and cannot do, even if they were in positions of authority. She taught me to challenge people's perceptions of me and my disability. In high school, a substitute calculus teacher refused to answer my question about our assignment and instead said, "I don't know why they mainstreamed you anyway. You shouldn't be in this class." I immediately asked her to repeat herself; I wanted to be sure I had heard her correctly. She replied, "You heard me." I said, "Yes, I did, and the principal will, too." I grabbed my crutches, stormed into the principal's office, and demanded to see her, tears of anger streaming down my face. I told the principal what had happened. Ultimately, the principal terminated the substitute teacher.

I realize the goal of this book is to help parents understand how they can better equip their children to handle life with a disability. Nonetheless, my desire would be for all the parents of children with disabilities to meet my parents.

~

TAMEEKA HUNTER *is the ADAPTS (Access Disabled Assistance Programs for Tech Students) program coordinator for the Georgia Institute of Technology where she provides accommodations for students with disabilities on Georgia Tech's campus. Prior to working at Tech, she was appointed to work as the disability affairs coordinator for the City of Atlanta, Mayor's Office. She earned a B.A. in Business Administration from Georgia State University and is an active member of Delta Sigma Theta Sorority, Inc. She currently serves as a board mem-*

ber on the Governor's Council for Developmental Disabilities, the Georgia Americans with Disabilities Act Exchange, and Full Radius Dance (a dance troupe that features dancers with and without disabilities). Tameeka is a twenty-nine-year-old female with cerebral palsy; she uses Canadian forearm crutches to walk. In her spare time, Tameeka enjoys reading, cooking, shopping, and cultural events.

GO FOR IT!

Douglas N. Little

"Y OUR SON IS A JUVENILE DIABETIC. *You will have to give him a daily insulin injection, regulate all his meals and snacks, and monitor his activity. Make sure he gets enough activity—yet doesn't overdo it.*"

Such words place much responsibility on parents. They push many parents to wrap their wings around their children, protecting them and keeping them safe. But, in doing so, many opportunities and experiences that life has to offer are eliminated.

Fortunately for one little, blonde-haired, blue-eyed boy, his parents took a different approach. When he was six and his classmates were going out to play tag and kickball, he asked, "Can I? Can I?" His parents, with instructions to the teachers to keep a watchful eye, said, "Go for it!"

When he was eight and the other 4-H kids were going to overnight camp, he asked, "Can I? Can I?" With instructions to the camp nurse to make sure he came in for his insulin injection every morning and to the kitchen staff to make sure he came in for his snacks, his parents said, "Go for it!"

When he was ten and his buddies were going out for the intramural basketball team, he asked, "Can I? Can I?" His parents, stashing cans of orange juice and sugar packets in his gym bag, said, "Go for it!"

When he was twelve and his older brothers and his buddies were going hunting, he asked, "Can I? Can I?" His parents, making sure he had candies and crackers in his pockets, said, "Go for it!"

In those early years, there were some times when the boy didn't listen to his body. And his parents didn't catch the signals quickly enough. As a result, he had some severe insulin reactions. Some were so severe that he was hospitalized for a week or more—to try to adjust his insulin and redo his meal plans, hoping to stabilize his diabetic condition. These were the times when his parents questioned their approach. But seeing the spunk and life in their son, they put the question aside. Through his teen years and early adulthood, they gave him the same advice whenever opportunities presented themselves: "Go for it!" And he did.

In his mid-twenties, the long-term complications of diabetes began to set in. He had partial renal failure because his kidneys weren't filtering correctly. And the nerves in his hands and feet began to fail, leaving him with numbness, prickly feelings, or just terrible pain.

But it was his eyes that took the brunt of the damage. Over a seventeen-month period, even after undergoing extensive laser treatments and surgeries, he went from being perfectly sighted to being totally blind. He was going to have to relearn many things including some basic daily living skills.

When the opportunity to go to a residential school for the blind came, although he was still in pain and deeply depressed, he could hear the words of his parents in the back of his mind, "Go for it! Go for it!"

With the skills learned at the school, using adaptations and adjustments, trial and error, and the "Go for it" attitude, he would overcome many of the challenges put before him. To this day, he lives a full, productive, and independent life.

How do I know so much about the little, blonde-haired, blue-eyed boy? That boy was me. I was the one who became a diabetic at age three, ripped and tore on the playgrounds, ran the mountains at camp, played on the basketball court, and pushed through the briars in the hunting fields. I was the one with the parents who said, "Go for it!" when new and different opportunities presented themselves. And, I am the one who went blind at twenty-six and had to relearn many tasks.

Did my parents do right? Some forty years later, because of the many complications of diabetes that have occurred, my parents question whether their approach was a good one. They wonder whether they should have reined me in, monitored me more closely, and been a little more protective—keeping me safe, essentially from myself.

Did my parents do right? Through the years, I have had friends with diabetes, who, like me, were diagnosed at a very early age. Several of these friends had very protective, perhaps overprotective, parents who didn't let them play tag and kickball, or go to camp, or play basketball, or go hunting. They didn't let them grab all the joy out of life. In short, their parents didn't let them live. And now, they can't—they have passed away. Did my parents do right?

Yes, without doubt, without regret—my parents did right!

Now I am a parent myself. When I heard those words, "Your son is a juvenile diabetic. You will have to give him a daily insulin injection, regulate all his meals and snacks, and monitor his activity. Make sure he gets enough activity—yet doesn't overdo it," I knew it was a tremendous responsibility. But, I also knew that when an opportunity presented itself and my son asked, "Can I? Can I?"— my answer would be just like my parents', "Go for it!"

≈

DOUGLAS LITTLE *lives in State College, Pennsylvania, with his wife, Debbie. Doug has two children, Ryan, seventeen, and Carrie, three. He is a stay-at-home dad. Doug is a motivational speaker, giving pre-*

sentations for elementary and middle school students, local univer-
sity undergraduates, professional organizations, and community serv-
ice groups. His message of perseverance, adjustment, and adaptation
are expressed through stories of his life experiences as a community
member with diabetes and blindness. He continues to enjoy hunting
and writing about his hunting experiences, watching sports of all
kinds, and reading mystery novels.

TAPPING MY POTENTIAL

Jamie C. Ray

I AM AN ATTORNEY, licensed to practice law in the Commonwealth of Pennsylvania and the state of New Jersey. I live and work in Philadelphia. I am happy to say that I am now what many people call a "Philadelphia Lawyer." I am also a woman with cerebral palsy, a developmental disability that impairs my walking and balance.

When I was in sixth grade, I told my parents I was going to be a lawyer. They thought I would change my mind. After all, I was only eleven. I didn't. At sixteen, I informed my mother that I was going to learn to tap dance for my high school musical. I did. I developed an unusual skill. I can readily describe and identify almost any tap step. The law and the stage are where I find passion.

One of the best things about my parents is that they always allowed me to pursue these interests, regardless of my disability. It didn't matter whether these things looked "possible" or "smart" to an outsider, or many times, even to them.

I practice law because I am driven to do so. It allows me to put all of my energies into ensuring fairness and equality. I can't think of any other field that provides such an awesome and unique opportunity. I can't imagine another career. But, if for some unthinkable reason I couldn't practice law, I would sing and dance on Broadway.

In high school, I fell in love with the stage, and especially musical theater. The stage is a place where, much like a courtroom, fairness and equality are alive. It is electric. For me, these principles live on stage because it is the one place where I can literally choose not to be a person with a disability. I am only disabled if the character I play is disabled. This ability to make my own choices is of fundamental importance.

I remember very vividly asking my mother to sign a permission slip so I could take tap dancing lessons after school. The spring musical was *42nd Street*, and the word in the halls was that everyone who didn't know how to tap better start learning! The lessons would be free, but we would need to buy shoes. The necessary shoes were "character shoes." Standard character shoes for adults are made with about a one-and-a-half inch heel. Immediately at issue: heels and cerebral palsy do not mix! I am sure my mother thought this fact would quickly end the discussion of tap dance lessons. However, I would not be deterred. I spoke to the teacher, and she did some research. She found that a pair of tap shoes with flat heels could be special ordered for me. (Today, I might call those shoes a "reasonable accommodation." Then, I didn't even know what the words meant.) With this new information, I again presented the permission slip to my mother. She was skeptical, but she signed—and I began to tap.

I didn't just tap at class. I tapped every day in our basement. Over and over, I repeated the basic steps—the shuffle, the flap, and the time step, in an effort to pattern my brain and get the right messages to my feet. I don't remember missing a single dance class, and thanks to my parents, I competed in the dance audition for Penn Manor Productions' *42nd Street*.

I will never forget the audition. It was a one-night-only chance to dance in the line. About two hours beforehand, an ice storm started. It was dangerous, and probably stupid, but my parents drove me to that audition anyway. It took well over an hour to drive what should have taken thirty minutes. They drove because they knew this was my dream. They drove, even though they knew I didn't have a snowball's chance in hell of dancing in that show. To this day, the only person I have publicly tap danced for is my grandmother.

This story illustrates two things I learned from my parents that are fundamental to me becoming a successful adult with a disability and that I believe every parent of a person with a disability should know. First, the only truly impossible dream is the one you *choose* not to pursue. Second, achieving success is a very personal journey. The steps you take in getting there shape the end result. Their importance should not be overlooked or underestimated.

If you asked me in high school what experiences would impact my career, I doubt I would have mentioned learning to tap dance. Only now, I see that the tools I took from that experience have helped me succeed in a world that is not always as welcoming as the theater department at Penn Manor High School.

Before I entered my freshman year of college, I had my first real experience with "disability stereotype." In this case, it involved the mistaken belief that there is a direct connection between the function of one's feet and the mental capacity of one's brain. I was told by a physician that "becoming a lawyer is a lofty goal for someone like you." Luckily, a friend of mine showed me a law called the Rehabilitation Act and, most important, introduced me to a part of this law called vocational rehabilitation. This federal law is designed to level the playing field for people with disabilities. It provides the same fairness and equality that I experience when playing a role on stage—it, too, is based upon choice. Until then I thought the practice of law would involve me prosecuting accused rapists, drug dealers, and murderers. In the Rehabilitation Act, I found something new and different. I found another tool to help me prove that doctor wrong. I was empowered by my discovery.

Today, I am the managing attorney at the Center for Disability Law & Policy (CDLP), which provides advocacy and assists individuals with disabilities throughout Pennsylvania in protecting their legal rights under the Rehabilitation Act and the Americans with

Disabilities Act (ADA). My work provides me the opportunity to help others with disabilities as they work toward their own vocational goals. I am proud of my role in this process. And I value the opportunity to be an example of how vocational rehabilitation is an important and necessary part of enabling individuals with disabilities to become independent and integrated into the workplace and community. Essential to my work are the principles of fairness and equality.

Follow your dreams, be guided by your own choices, personalize your successes, and use the law as a tool of empowerment. With these fundamentals in mind, there is no such thing as a "lofty goal."

~

JAMIE RAY *is the managing attorney at the Center for Disability Law & Policy (CDLP), Philadelphia, Pennsylvania. She is a 1999 graduate of Temple University School of Law, where she was a note/comment editor for the* Temple Political & Civic Rights Law Reviews. *She received her undergraduate degree in 1995 from York College of Pennsylvania and is a 1992 graduate of Penn Manor High School. She is admitted to practice law in both Pennsylvania and New Jersey.*

Jamie is the current vice-chairperson of the Pennsylvania Rehabilitation Council as well as vice-chairperson of the Pennsylvania Bar Association's Delivery of Legal Services to Persons with Disabilities Committee. She is actively involved in the Pennsylvania Bar Association's Women in the Profession Committee.

In addition to her legal pursuits, she is a member of a Philadelphia-based comedy improvisation group "Too Many Lawyers." She is the daughter of Randall and Barbara Ray of Lancaster County, Pennsylvania.

THE HAND THAT YOU'RE DEALT

Jimmy Dinsmore

THE PERSON THAT I AM NOW reflects the struggles and tribulations that I endured growing up with spina bifida in an otherwise normal family

Most of those tribulations came within my family. My older sister did not have a disability and truly embraced her little brother. However, I couldn't help but think that there was always some resentment toward me. After all, I was "special" and required more of my mom's and dad's attention. Plus, on family outings, I slowed us down a bit. It definitely wasn't easy to be my sister. When we went out in public, people would stare. It wasn't easy on me, and I'm sure my sister was embarrassed by me. It would only be natural. Even today, I haven't adjusted to the people who stare at me in public.

Growing up in the Midwest in an average middle-class family made me stick out like a sore thumb. I was the only kid with a disability in my elementary school or in my neighborhood. This elevated me to minor "celebrity" status within my school and neighborhood. Everyone knew who I was. I used that to my advantage. I actually enjoyed it. Everyone in school usually struggles to be well known and it was just happening naturally for me. I didn't care why—I was "popular." Even today, I can go back to my school and people will recognize me. Or people I went to school with, who I haven't seen in years, still recognize me—simply because of the way I walk. It's both a curse and a gift.

As a boy, I often felt angry about why I ended up with my disability. I questioned God and throughout my life have battled with my faith. Why would a just and fair God give this disability to an innocent baby? I never asked for it.

I later learned the reason why I was chosen. God picked me because He knew I could handle it. He also knew that it would help shape me into the person that I am. In this way, it was a gift from Him. More times than not though, it seemed like a curse. If it wasn't for the love, support, and advice of my parents, I would probably still believe it was a curse.

Growing up with a disability was very challenging. My feelings got hurt on a regular basis, almost every day. Childhood can be cruel for anyone; it's that much harder for someone with a disability. The only way to persevere through the teasing is to have the support of good friends and family.

The biggest source of strength for me was my mother. She instilled one very important thing in me that is important for all people with disabilities to have—knowledge of my limitations. I remember as a little boy telling my mom that I wanted to be a fireman or a cowboy. She encouraged me, but she also reminded me of the reality that if I were to do so, it would be more challenging because of my disability. That was the key. She didn't say I couldn't be anything I wanted. But, at the same time, she kept me grounded. I do have physical limitations. Accepting that fact is a big step toward being well adjusted.

Once you are well adjusted, you begin to stand up for yourself and educate people about your disability. Getting to this stage is wonderful. One perfect example of this for me occurred in ninth grade—turbulent times for any young teenager.

I was in the locker room after gym class (a naturally uncomfortable situation for me). The "bully" who hounded me throughout junior high school was at it again. He kept calling me "peg leg" and imitating the way I walked. I heard "peg leg," "peg leg" over and over. Finally, I lost it. I took off my plastic orthotic leg brace and smacked him over the head with it. I told him, "I just hit you over the head with my peg leg and I'm standing here on both legs before you. So clearly, I don't have a peg leg."

Gasps and worry raced through the locker room. What is he doing, they wondered. Feeling humiliated, the bully began to get confrontational. Then the most amazing thing happened. All of those ninth graders, of various sizes and builds, stood in front of me with their arms crossed, blocking the bully from me. I had earned all of their respect and put the bully in his place. From that moment on, things were different at school for me. Respect, even for people with disabilities, is not given—it's earned.

Despite my newfound respect, I still wanted nothing more than to be like every other kid in my school. To take away from the obviousness of my disability, I became the class clown. I figured if I grabbed the spotlight in other ways, it would decrease the staring and whispering.

Although I did not realize it, I was developing a sense of who I was and where I fit into society. I adjusted quickly to high school and within my community. I believed that I was no different from anyone else—and in many ways that was true.

All of these realizations and triumphs would not have been possible without my mom, dad, and sister. Their support was invaluable. Most important of all, they treated me like a normal kid. I got punished or praised like a normal kid. While there was something special about me, my parents still treated me like they would a son without a disability. At the time, I didn't always appreciate it. Now, as an adult, I totally do.

Every person is special in their own way. I walk with a major limp and have a disability. Some people have bad vision and need to wear thick glasses. Other people are born with big noses. All of these things sculpt who we are. We can't do anything about it but accept it and embrace it.

In life, you either accept the hand that you're dealt or you give up. Giving up is never an option. Live the life that you want, regardless of the hand that you're dealt. This is all anyone, a person with a disability or not, can hope for.

∾

JIMMY DINSMORE *is a thirty-year-old working for a suburban newspaper in Cincinnati, Ohio, as an editor. He was born with spina bifida and has had thirteen surgeries to date. Unlike most people with spina bifida, he is actually ambulatory. He has difficulty walking or standing for long periods of time and does so with a significant limp. But he can do it.*

Just last year, Jimmy and his wife celebrated the birth of their perfectly healthy and beautiful little girl. That was truly the most wonderful thing that has happened in his life, says Jimmy. Fatherhood, along with walking, were two things he was told would never be possible. He proved "them" wrong. Already in life, he has climbed Mt. Massada in Israel, seen the world, and interviewed numerous celebrities for his job. It's been a wonderful, fulfilling life, and there's plenty more to see and do!

ALIEN OR ACTIVIST? A WOMAN IN SEARCH OF A BIG LIFE

Laureen Summers

I WAS BORN in New York City on August 24, 1947, into a middle-class Jewish family. It was one month and twenty-one days after a rancher in Roswell, New Mexico, found a wreckage of a strange craft in one of his sheep pastures. The U.S. Army Air Force identified it as a flying saucer, sparking years of mystery, conspiracy theories, and allegations of cover-ups. (In 1998, "Roswell," a teenage drama series, fascinated young minds searching for evidence of people coming from an alien world.)

Perhaps my birth following so closely after this historic event was no coincidence. I emerged—an alien to the doctors, a normal baby to my parents. The story I was told was that I was born not breathing. Six minutes without oxygen alters the brain functions of a baby. By the time I got enough, and perhaps too much, oxygen to start breathing, my body was affected. Some of the sensitive brain tissues that control movement were damaged. I would always have difficulty with fine motor coordination and my speech would be slow and sometimes unintelligible.

Cerebral palsy and its causes were unknown in the late 1940s. An old-fashioned doctor, whom her mother had chosen for her, treated my mom. She had had a viral infection and phlebitis in her last trimester of pregnancy and had an RH negative blood type. It is unclear whether any of these conditions contributed to mine. When I showed some spasticity in my movements, my parents thought it would eventually disappear. My grandmother finally noticed I wasn't following a normal pattern of development. At four months, I couldn't hold my head up or sit by myself. At six months, I didn't crawl. My movements were chaotic. I drooled.

My mother took me to various doctors, hoping for rational answers about my condition. The first doctor we saw handled me roughly. I cried. He ignored me, telling my mother I was a hopeless case. The second doctor said I would never walk. When I was two years old, a cousin of my mother's, who was practicing medicine in Montreal, visited us and diagnosed my symptoms as cerebral palsy. Another doctor, an expert in the field, recommended that I begin therapy three times a week. Physical therapy would strengthen my legs and help me to walk. Speech therapy would help me learn to speak more clearly. Occupational therapy would improve the coordination of my hands.

Images of my childhood pass through my mind from time to time. I had good friends, went to school, and had a decent family life. But I can't remember getting the reassurance I must have wanted that everything would be OK. My family seemed uncomfortable discussing things like feelings or my struggle to understand my own disability.

My mom would take me to doctors, often without telling me where we were going. We would get in the car on some pretext and wind up in front of a medical building. I was terrified and wondered why I was not given any information about what would happen to me. My mom just wanted to protect me. She knew I would be scared and confused. But I began to believe that no one would ever be completely truthful with me. I felt I always would have to fight for the right to my own opinion, especially about myself.

Although I was encouraged to do all the things every other child my age did, it seemed as if no one had any really big expectations of me. I remember my parents telling me that all I had to do in life was to just get by. All around me were adults, my parents' friends, who had done amazing things with their lives. They were recognized for their contributions in business, education, writing, and the arts. Listening to their conversations about ideas, life, and dreams, made me want to do much more than just get by.

I rebelled as soon as I could, often doing the things I was told not to. I was determined to prove I could do whatever I wanted, despite the cautionary tones with which my parents spoke. My parents were so careful with me. I wanted to be rough and tough like the kids in my neighborhood. They were smart, interesting, and full of life. I vowed that my life would be as exciting as theirs was.

It's difficult being a parent. One truly wants the absolute best for one's child at all times. But parents often confuse their needs with those of their children's. When a disability is involved, parents are often more cautious and more protective. The world at large is often insensitive and cruel to a person with a disability. The tendency of any parent is to shelter the child from this harshness. Even now when I ride the subway or go shopping or to a museum, or anywhere a crowd tends to be, I wish my mother was with me to help me cope with the strange stares and unspoken questions that seem so directly targeted at me. I wish she could have made me laugh—doing everything she could to contradict the seriousness and fear that can pervade the environment when a person with a disability is around. And I wish I could have been reassured, over and over and over, that, despite my limitations, I was still a person with talents who could have a wonderful and rich life.

It's not that one forgets about, or ignores, the difficult parts of disability. It's very important to pay attention to medical and therapeutic needs. It's crucial to insist on the best education one can get. But, in order to resolve all these important things, I believe that support and positive encouragement are absolutely necessary.

In my work now, as manager of an internship program for college students with disabilities, I have discovered over and over that the most successful students are the ones whose families have fought for them, despite the warnings from doctors, counselors, and teachers. These parents knew that their children were smart and could persevere. They knew that having a disability is no easy matter, but it did not preclude everything. They worked hard, as my parents did, to find the right therapy, the right doctors, and the right schools. They spent quality time with their families and made trips and vacations accessible and fun for everyone. And, not only did their children succeed in their education and in finding their career paths, but they also learned how to contradict any heavy seriousness that threatened to surround them. They know how to have a good time.

I fought for high expectations. When I became involved with disability organizations and disability activists, I was amazed that the expectations for people like myself were sometimes still low. Too much attention is given to the negatives—the low employment rate, the deep prejudicial attitudes, and the lack of accessible and affordable housing. No one gives enough attention to encouraging our talents; no one is pushing us to realize our dreams. No one is moving us forward to discover our own uniqueness. It feels like we still have to settle for less than our own ideals. It sometimes seems as if no one is really rooting for and cheering us on. In our eagerness to challenge the able-bodied world around us, we often forget to challenge each other.

Was I really born an alien? I don't really know. Perhaps it is alien to some that a child with a disability can actually grow up to do amazing things, despite all the needs surrounding a disability that one has to think about. But having the necessary supports—good friends and family who provide encouragement and trust—makes all the difference.

Did I get my big, full, wonderful life? I believe I have a great start. I have a wonderful family of my own—a marvelous husband of twenty-eight years and a fabulous nineteen-year-old daughter. I work full-time at a job I love. I have close friends around me. I have gone hiking and hot-air ballooning. I've wandered alone in strange cities and ridden one of the world's tallest Ferris wheels. I am a weaver of wall hangings. I work on disability issues. I love being with people and having time to be alone. And, yes, at the enchanting age of fifty-five, I still want everything I do to be exciting, productive, and fun!

≈

LAUREEN SUMMERS *is program associate for the Project on Science, Technology, and Disability at the American Association for the Advancement of Science and has been associated with the Project since 1991. Since 1996, she has been the project manager of the AAAS* ENTRY POINT! *program. She holds a B.A. from the College on the Potomac and has taken additional coursework at George Washington University. She is the coeditor of the* AAAS Resource Directory of Scientists and Engineers with Disabilities, *3rd ed. (AAAS, 1995), and the book* Access Science: Themes and Variations *(AAAS and the National Easter Seals Society, 1998). She has also contributed to* Roadmaps and Rampways *(AAAS, 2001).*

A woman with cerebral palsy, Laureen has worked in the disability field for twenty-three years, including working as a peer counselor in Independent Living Centers and as a media specialist at the National Rehabilitation Information Center.

GIVING OUR CHILDREN ROOTS AND WINGS

Barbara Ramnaraine

A S A VERY YOUNG CHILD, I knew that I did not see what other children saw. But my parents, my teachers, and the other adults who cared about me treated me like any other child.

I was legally blind from birth and lost the remainder of my vision at age twenty-seven. No one seemed to know that I had the hereditary disease retinitis pigmentosa. Only when my second child was born did we discover that he too was legally blind, manifesting the same symptoms that I had displayed.

Somehow, my parents knew how to bring up a child who had limited vision. The lessons that I learned from them and from my experiences as a child with a disability are what I have used in parenting my son.

Your Child Is a Whole Person

I am who I am because of—not in spite of—my disability. The way I relate to others and the way I view the world are affected by my blindness. Being blind is not the most important part of who I am. The reality of our abilities and disabilities needs to be kept in balance by those who love and care for us. Coddling, smothering, and infantilizing are destructive. Wise parents learn to see their children as whole people, with gifts to share and limitations to accept.

As the oldest, I was expected to help care for my younger siblings. I had jobs to do around the house. Like most kids, I tried to get out of my jobs, but "I can't see" was not an acceptable way to accomplish this. Because my parents had high expectations for me, I learned to have high expectations for myself.

I was always encouraged and never belittled. My limits were expanded because my parents cared enough to challenge me. I did not realize until adulthood that my parents were sometimes afraid for my safety and shadowed me when I set off for school or on an errand. Because they exhibited no noticeable apprehension, I did not learn to be afraid.

Love, Do Not Pity

Love sets us free; pity imprisons us. Jim, my legally blind son, loved baseball and wanted to play it at school when he was nine years old. He became the catcher on his team. Yes, he was smacked by the bat when he crouched too close to the plate. But he played, and he grew from that experience.

During college, Jim wanted to spend a January term abroad. He was apprehensive and asked me what I thought. I told him that all fears must be acknowledged and confronted if we are to live free of them and that I would support him in whatever decision he made. He enjoyed London enormously.

Encourage Dreams

When I was twelve, I began to dream about being a doctor, just like my parents and my favorite uncle. I am certain that my parents understood that medical school, residency, and the practice of medicine would be nearly impossible for me. In a few years, I came to the same conclusion. It was my decision and not their declaration that accounted for my change in career path. I had discovered other interests that were more appropriate to my abilities and disability. Lovingly and carefully, parents can help shape their children's dreams. Hopes for the future are an important part of growing up, and a life without dreams is impoverished.

Avoid Isolation

Parents and children need friends. It can be difficult for a child with a disability to make friends. I was the last child chosen for teams and games, and I remember kids pointing at me and saying, "She's hard of seeing." At age five, I stole money from my mom to buy candy for my classmates. I knew I wanted to be liked and how bad it felt to be alone.

Children need to become comfortable with their disability. When parents accept their child's disability and treat it simply as one aspect of their child's life, the child will also become comfortable. When children are encouraged to be open with others about the equipment they use and about their particular daily routines, everyone involved will be more at ease. It is equally important for children to acknowledge and share their abilities.

Parenting a child with a disability can be time-consuming, energy-draining, and isolating. Expand your family to include neighbors, other parents with children with disabilities, and friends from church and work. Arrange for respite care when you need it. Make friends with adults with whom you can be someone other than "a parent of a child with a disability." Learn to ask for help and to take time for yourself. You cannot help your child if you are not healthy and whole.

In my opinion, independence is much overrated. Interdependence is a much healthier and more enjoyable way of life. The maxim "it takes a village to raise a child" is particularly true for raising a child with a disability.

Teach Advocacy

Parents discover early that they must become advocates on behalf of their child. When our son was six, we wanted to enroll him in a school that had each child take a paper and pencil intelligence test requiring visual skills. Our legally blind son tested as having below normal intelligence. We had him tested by a reliable psychologist, and our son proved to be above normal in intelligence. We enrolled him elsewhere.

No one knows your child as well as you do. Equip yourselves with resources. Contact an organization dedicated to your child's disability. Seek the advice of professionals. Talk with other parents and share solutions that have worked. Trust yourself, and do not be intimidated by professionals.

When your child is old enough, begin teaching the advocacy skills that you have learned. Children are empowered when they are able to tell others what they need. Being assertive is an important tool for children and parents.

Try to Be Fair

I learned as an adult that my younger sister has always resented the amount of time our parents gave to me. From her perspective, I received an inordinate amount of their love and attention. Whether or not this is accurate, she has been angry with my parents and alienated from me.

Some parents may, of necessity, spend more time with their child with a disability. But it is not good for anyone to have the child be the center of everyone's attention.

To the extent possible, children can be given responsibilities as well as privileges. A disability is never an excuse for obnoxious behavior or for shirking chores. All children can learn to be considerate of, and helpful to, their brothers and sisters. If these lessons are not taught early on, the adult child will lack social skills and be self-centered. Behavior tolerated in a family may not be tolerated by the world.

Plan for the Future

Children with disabilities need to be prepared for a life beyond their family. During their development, they need to learn daily living skills. I was not taught such skills when I could have easily learned them. I lived at home through college and soon afterward married and moved away. I was not prepared for leaving the family or marriage. I had never dated and was socially immature. Eventually I acquired the skills I needed, but it was a struggle for several years. My parents were negligent about this part of my education.

My son lived away from home for college and did not marry until several years after he had completed his education and begun working. Unlike me, he had acquired skills early in his life that enabled him to function more comfortably and effectively outside the family.

Preparing for the future is different for each child. Sometimes, it may mean looking for a group home and setting aside funds for a child's care after parents die. For others, it means providing the encouragement for the child to find suitable schooling or employment so that she or he is prepared to leave home. In my opinion, it should never mean expecting siblings to assume care of their brother or sister with a disability.

Early planning can avoid a great deal of anxiety. A friend with a son with moderate cerebral palsy and mental retardation began thinking about her son's future when he was in his twenties. Although she told me that it was the hardest thing she had ever done, she, her husband, and their son began looking for a group home for him. Today, he lives in a wonderful, supportive setting; enjoys friends and many activities; and maintains a loving relationship with his parents and his brother.

Although parents always worry about them, they must give their children roots and wings. When parents do this, they will enjoy a life of their own knowing that their adult children are living successfully, productively, and happily.

Rejoice and Be Thankful

Parenting is difficult and rewarding. Parenting a child with a disability can be more difficult and more rewarding. Parents can find joy, rejoice in small victories, and be thankful for the gifts their children have to share as well as for failures that lead to new learning.

Children are adept at reading their parents' emotions. When parents are unhappy, worried, or discomforted by their child's disability, the child will absorb these emotions and blame themselves.

Living well with a disability requires fortitude, perseverance, and ingenuity. Acquiring and nurturing these qualities is easier when parents are supportive, encouraging, proud, and insightful—and when they keep a sense of humor and do not take themselves or their children too seriously.

Children with disabilities have much to teach about patience and the illusion of perfection. They live in the "now" and treasure small successes. These are traits to be valued and cultivated.

My parents gifted me with love and a desire to be the best that I could be. The lessons I learned from them I tried to pass on to my children. My wish for all children is that they be loved, find joy in life, and become the best that they can be.

∾

BARBARA RAMNARAINE *was born in 1934, the oldest of three children. She was legally blind from birth and lost the remainder of her vision when she was twenty-seven. She is a graduate of Macalester*

College, St. Paul, Minnesota, where she earned a B.A. in chemistry with a minor in English and education. She taught for three years in South Dakota and western Minnesota. She was married in 1951 and is the mother of three grown children. Her middle child, James, was born with the same hereditary disease (retinitis pigmentosa) that she has.

In 1984, Barbara was ordained in the Episcopal Church as a permanent deacon. She is currently the coordinator of the Episcopal Disability Network and serves as deacon at St. Paul's Episcopal Church in Minneapolis.

An enthusiastic gardener and an avid reader, Barbara now lives in her childhood home. Two of her best friends are Micah, a twelve-year-old Samoyed, and Beau, an eleven-year-old white German shepherd.

4

SEXUALITY

RELATIONSHIP REALISM

Jennifer Malatesta

"NINETY-NINE.NINE [99.9] PERCENT of guys would not want to date, let alone marry, someone in a wheelchair." My well-meaning mother offered this unsolicited assessment to me during my impressionable preteen years. Eleven years of marriage and two children later, most people think I have proven my mother wrong and that this statement should not still be replaying itself in my mind every day. But it does.

My parents, like many others, thought it was best to prepare me for the harsh realities of the world by focusing on the more dire possibilities for my future. Life is tough, and they wanted to make sure I did not enter into it clinging to fairy tale fantasies of love, joy, and Prince Charming. They knew that many opportunities most young women take for granted would only be acquired through a lot of extra work and determination. They strove to build up my emotional armor by encouraging me to prepare for the worst.

I can understand why they felt the need to "toughen me up." Living a life with a physical disability is not easy, and it should not be presented as such. Not only do some people still harbor overt prejudices against persons with disabilities, but unconscious biases exist in even the most benevolent people. These biases become especially apparent when a person, who does not have a disability, willingly decides to start a relationship with a person who does. Otherwise kindhearted friends and family shower praises on the individual without a disability for his or her seemingly altruistic and self-sacrificing intentions, but, inevitably, a dose of their version of realism is offered: "Have you thought this through?" "What if the disability progresses?" "And, what about having children?" All these are commonly poised questions. They are one of the realities of dating someone with a disability, and such attitudes have stalled or stopped many love affairs.

Luckily, the number of people who would never consider dating a person simply because they are in a wheelchair is less than my parents had construed. When discussing the topic of dating with a young person with a disability, there must be a balance. Attention needs to be paid to what the individual can offer to a relationship, not what he or she is lacking. He or she needs to be encouraged to develop personal interests, hobbies, and knowledge, so that a well-rounded personality can be offered to the world. It can even be pointed out that being a person with a disability has its own advantages in courtship. It often "weeds out" potential mates who choose their partners based on superficial attributes. For example, I will never live up to the American prototype of physical beauty; but I also do not want to be married to someone who bases his affection on fleeting visceral attraction.

An overly negative view can be devastating to a person's sense of self-worth, with or without a disability. When a person hears that his or her physical attributes are the sole determining factors of their dating potential, the individual may start to base his or her self-image on these traits—even though the ideal of beauty set up by society is unobtainable for many.

To counteract society's overemphasis on fitting into an idealized Hollywood mold, many parents try to encourage their children to focus on others' inner beauty instead of outward appearances. Why then, if a child has a disability, do parents imply that this child's entire being and dating potential is predetermined by his or her physical appearance? Such a message can be more disabling than any physical limitation.

Having a negative self-image can cause people with disabilities to settle for less-than-desirable—even dangerous—mates. During my time in the dating scene, I contemplated marrying everyone from a man I was not attracted to at all to a man with a photo album filled with pictures of his female conquests. I even thought about being the chaste matriarchal figurehead in a "family" with my gay friend and his lover. I also toyed with the idea of marrying many different "druggies" and "burn-outs." After all, I was convinced I only had one-tenth of 1 percent of the male population to consider. I had not been encouraged to be choosy. Fortunately, I escaped these situations and married a very caring and giving man, who views me as an equal partner with valuable opinions.

Others are not so fortunate. If fed a constant diet of unfavorable expectations, future relationships can become tragic, self-fulfilling prophecies. If people with disabilities are led to believe that they cannot expect loving relationships, they may become willing to accept emotional, verbal, or physical abuse as a twisted legacy.

Once people with disabilities are in detrimental relationships, it can be harder for them to escape. When I got married, I immediately lost all my government-sponsored benefits for my personal care. My case is not an isolated one by any means. In fact, couples I know have forgone a "traditional" legal marriage so that the partner with a disability can continue to receive personal attendant and in-home nursing care. In other situations, a married person with a disability has no other option but to rely on the spouse as the only caregiver. If this caregiver starts to neglect or abuse the partner, the person with the disability is trapped in the marriage. Separating from an abusive spouse may leave the individual with a disability without personal care options—forcing the individual into an institution. If children are involved, the person with a disability may face the threat of losing custody of the children to the abusive partner or a government agency.

Even in healthy marital relationships, the excess baggage of not feeling worthy of a spouse's love and care can lead to depression and jealousy. Well-meaning individuals often unintentionally make statements that reinforce the idea that the individual with a disability is really a "burden" to the spouse. Statements like "your husband is a saint," however true they may be, always stab me with a twinge of guilt. It is not easy to be viewed as someone's "cross to bear." Although it is true that my husband made a very life-altering decision to marry a person in a wheelchair, I, in my brighter moments, like to believe that people can see the positive contributions I make to our relationship. On darker days, the sense of dread I feel that I have somehow doomed my husband to a mediocre, even frustrating, existence can send me swirling into a debilitating depression. When it seems like society constantly questions why your partner chose you, you can begin to question your partner's intentions as well.

Jealousy can also come into play. Friends of mine with disabilities have lived in constant anxiety when they were in relationships. Anytime a person expressed admiration for their significant other, they were convinced that the person was out to steal their loved one. Each time they encountered a person who better fit the "standards" of beauty, they felt inferior as a partner. Any person with any superficial advantage was viewed as a threat. Since they could not understand the positive attributes that attracted their partner to them in the first place—mainly because these attributes were played down by friends and relatives while growing up—they could not appreciate why their partner would choose to remain with them. This constant second-guessing can be very detrimental to any partnership.

I am glad that my parents did not present me with a happy fantasy world where everything would work out fine and I would be guaranteed to meet my own knight in shining armor. I also realize that it must have been quite a shift in their expectations to watch their daughter, who was not expected to live past the age of two years, grow up, date, marry, and have children of her own. Nonetheless, I do wish my parents had presented the possibilities of intimate relationships in a more balanced and positive way. Life with a disability is more difficult in some ways, but it needs to be pointed out that everyone has some sort of disability. Some are just more obvious than others. Everyone has gifts and creativity to offer to others in loving relationships. Each and every person is worthy of love, and no physical, emotional, or mental disability should preclude it.

~

JENNIFER MALATESTA *is a thirty-two-year-old wife and mother of two girls. She was born with a form of muscular dystrophy called spinal muscular atrophy. At the time of her diagnosis, her parents were told not to expect their daughter to live past the age of two. She proved this prediction wrong by graduating with honors in 1988 from Notre Dame Academy High School in Toledo, Ohio, and then graduating summa cum laude in 1992 from Wright State University in Dayton, Ohio. She met her husband, Lee, at Wright State in 1990, and they married the next year. After a difficult birth experience with her daughter Emili in 1993, Jennifer "retired" the next year for medical reasons. Three years later, she had her second daughter, Ravyn, without any complications. Since her retirement, she has focused her energies on writing and motherhood. She lives in Cincinnati, Ohio, with her family.*

CODE OF SILENCE

Anonymous

I'M LOOKING OUT THE WINDOW *at my blossoming cherry tree. Its first year in bloom and I'm in love with its grace. Pale pink flowers jostle for every spot on the small limbs, the losing blossoms scattering into a circle around the trunk. To the left sit the few daffodils, which the squirrels left me after a hard winter. My sight, though, always returns to a mass of tan spread out immediately inside the road. . . .*

I remember a simple statement made years ago by my psychology professor, a casual remark that nevertheless touched the empty spot in me, the hole I've never been able to fill. He said, "I think the worst thing in the world is to want something you can never have."

I wonder, if I had had a traditional family, would the empty spot have been filled? Maybe there's a wholeness that comes with children, and now, at forty-four, it's not likely that such completion will ever be mine. Many times I have asked myself why I've remained childless, why the thought of children scares me and has always seemed like a goal not quite within reach. I have read countless recollections by couples who have subjected themselves to every intrusion to have their own children, but I don't relate. All of my siblings have children. It just seemed to be a natural progression of their lives. We all graduated from college, married, and bought homes, but the similarities ended with the first births of nieces and nephews.

Looking back, I have to wonder whether the expectations of others were too powerful to overcome . . . in this one area of my life.

My childhood friends and I were experts at playing house, but I don't remember any adults saying to me, "When you're a mommy . . . " My parents, who separated when I was twelve, seemed to have had a pact to treat me "like all the other kids," but when it came to sex, they pushed their rule of equity aside. I see it now as a cultural characteristic that they could neither transcend nor trash, this refusal to accept the sexuality of individuals with disabilities. I have tried most of my life to ignore this insult, but still it eats at the edges of my dignity. When I realized my mother did not expect me to get married, much less have my own family, I concluded that she was as ignorant as the rest of the world. But it still tore at my heart.

I loved being feminine and having the attention of boys as much as my friends and sisters did. Although I was born with clubfeet and scoliosis, I never felt ugly, even during my teen years. But those years were also unnecessarily mysterious. My mother never told me about sex or prepared me for bodily transformations. This was during the 1970s, when few taboos remained, so I was able to learn what I needed to know from books and magazines. Everybody except my mom, so it seemed, was talking about sex. But even during that liberal era, sex was limited to people who were neither disabled nor deformed. Sex for the likes of me remained locked in whispers.

I'll never forget how crushed I was to learn that although my mother met my sexual development with silence, she was able to overcome her reticence enough to educate my sister about sex. Worse yet, she instructed my sister to repeat it to me. If I can pinpoint a time when a veil of impenetrable discomfort descended between my mom and me, this was probably it. Her silence ushered in a lifetime of my feeling shunned by her as a woman.

Eventually, it became clear that not only did my mother not expect me to marry, she did not want me to marry. Rather, after I graduated from college, she expected me to buy a house with her. Even after establishing myself in a job and an apartment, my mother still almost begged me to partner up with her in a house. I retained the dignity to be outraged by such expectations. What did she think I had been preparing for all my life? I had never been dependent, had always fought people who wanted to "baby" me. Now suddenly my growth as a woman and as an individual was, out of the blue, expected to shriek to a halt. Of course, not for one second did I consider living with my mother or anyone else in the family.

Eventually, circumstances forced my mother to admit that her youngest was going to embarrass the hell out of her and get married. I came to believe that my sexuality, in the end, simply embarrassed her. So great is the cultural taboo against sexual expression for anyone "outside the circle" that I've witnessed people redden in the face at the mere mention of my husband. But no amount of denial can abridge the symbol of marriage as a sexual bond; thus, short of disowning me, no one in the family could sidestep my sexuality. I'd have a ring on my finger. My mom finally stopped asking me to return home.

Yet after the wedding, when my husband and I had the effrontery to fantasize about children, we realized that even the mere possibility of our procreation opened up a new chapter in dealing with the discomfort of others. Although *his* family seemed to be quite comfortable with the idea, accepting the whole package of our partnership, my family recoiled in disapproval, and my mom seemed utterly speechless. Finally, she told me I couldn't be "serious." We did not speak for weeks. I'm sure part of my mother's terror stems from the thought of being seen with the now-wheelchair-mobile me pregnant. Whoever saw pregnant women in wheelchairs loose on the streets? Why, the whole world would know that I had had sex. And then . . . yes, and then what? What would happen except that we would all have someone else to love?

Relief swept through the family when I was in law school. Surely I wasn't crazy enough to contemplate a family during those difficult years. But then I had the nerve to divorce Jack and marry Todd, who craved his own child. This became known to my family, which had grown quite large. My family's reply, so uniform that I assumed it had been discussed, was and remains silence. The very subject has, in fact, ended many conversations. Just recently, for instance, I forgot myself for a moment and showed my mother a picture of a friend's new adopted daughter. My mother reluctantly glanced at the picture, her face settling into disapproval. I was crushed and felt foolish. I asked myself, could this person also be my loving mother? The woman who waited years for a grandchild and immersed herself in preparation for each birth? Who spent months of her life sewing wardrobes and making dolls and Halloween costumes for her cherished grandchildren?

Anyone who has looked into the eyes of another human and realized that there is something missing in those eyes—something withheld from their expression simply because of what you look like—knows the pain invoked can never be fully expressed or discarded. There is a unique quality of cruelty that accompanies the realization that although your family members may love children, *your* children are not welcome.

It hurts me not to be accepted as a whole human being by the people I have loved the most. How much closer we could have been as a family if only I had been extended the right to be me, fully actualized. Unfortunately, this refusal to share in my personhood will always be a wedge between my family and me, long past our reproductive years.

I return to the question, when was it that I was left behind? . . .

The mound of fur has opened his pink mouth in a huge yawn. Suddenly, his eyes grow immense and still. His tail begins to sweep the air and soon his body livens with joy as my husband's car pulls into the driveway and his daddy steps out. My beloved dog gallops to greet the most cherished of fathers.

This is my family, for now.

~

THE AUTHOR *of this essay prefers to be anonymous.*

MY MOTHER'S WARNINGS

Anne Abbott

EVERYTHING SEEMED SO SIMPLE when I was a child. I had a happy, well-adjusted childhood. Sure, I had cerebral palsy and had to have assistance with all of my daily needs, but I also had a family that loved me, supported me, and tried their best to give me as normal a life as possible. With them behind me, I felt as if I could do anything or become anybody I wanted. When I told them that I wanted to be a doctor or a nurse or an actress when I grew up, nobody made fun of my dreams or said that they were impossible. When I told them that some day I wanted to be a wife and mother, they would say, "That's nice, dear. I'm sure that'll happen one day for you if you really want it to."

I liked playing with other children. Since my older brother and I were very close, it seemed natural for me to be included in his circle of friends. When I went to a school for children with disabilities, I made friends with girls and boys my own age. My girlfriends and I played with our dolls, pretending that they were real people, living within a real family setting, acting out real family situations. Like other little girls, we were preparing ourselves for what we supposed our lives might be like when we grew up.

I had boyfriends, too. Like my girlfriends, some of the boys had disabilities and some were able-bodied. There were often romantic feelings between these boys and me. I had my first kiss on the lips from one boy when I was eight and then got "married" at age ten to another boy in my class. I was becoming aware of my sexuality.

When I reached my teens, everything seemed to change. Gone were the days of playing with dolls and the mock marriage ceremonies during recess. Overnight, the age of innocence had seemingly disappeared. The rules had suddenly changed. Everyone was becoming concerned about their body image, trying to fit in, trying to find their own place. Like other teenagers, we began to find fault with the way we looked, becoming overcritical at the sight of the slightest flaw. The people on television, in movies, and in the music industry didn't help. They seemed to be so beautiful, so perfect, so flawless. It seemed as if society and the media were saying that you had to look perfect in order to succeed in life. It didn't help that people with disabilities were rarely shown or mentioned, and, if they were, they were portrayed as helpless and asexual.

I felt terribly confused and inadequate during my teenage years. Unwittingly, my mother added to these feelings by trying to give me some advice. She told me to try not to become romantically interested in able-bodied boys because they would never want the responsibility of taking care of someone with cerebral palsy. It was her experience, she explained, that men liked to be taken care of, but they didn't particularly like to take care of someone else. I should stick to boys with cerebral palsy or other types of disabilities who would understand my needs. My mother wasn't trying to hurt me when she said this; she just wanted to save me from rejection.

Rejected I was—by both able-bodied boys and boys with disabilities! I found that a lot of boys with disabilities only wanted to become involved with able-bodied girls. They didn't want to stick to girls who happened to have disabilities; indeed, they didn't think they should have to. One boy explained, "You live with your disability every day of your life. Why would you want someone who's exactly like you to remind you of your own limitations?"

There were some, admittedly, who didn't care whether a girl was able-bodied or not. Unfortunately, I just never "clicked" with these guys. Either they weren't my type, or I wasn't theirs.

I learned that sometimes you can't help whom you're attracted to. Despite my mother's warnings, there were times when I tried to catch the attention of able-bodied men. I was like any other woman. If I saw a good-looking guy, I'd want to sit and talk to him, maybe even flirt with him. A lot of these guys liked me—but never in "that way." They said they just wanted to be friends.

It was unbelievably frustrating and demoralizing. I felt as if I were invisible, as if I were a nonperson. I felt as if society expected me to suppress my sexuality and act as if it didn't matter. Sexual intimacy was just something I would not, could not, do. There were also some people who assumed I was void of any type of sexuality to begin with and needed to be protected from any kind of sexual relationships.

Outwardly, I was the same person I'd always been—cheerful, outgoing, optimistic. But inside I began to feel angry and resentful of these attitudes, of all the restrictions that were put upon me. I just couldn't understand what had happened to my life. As a child I was included in all aspects of life; now, I was excluded from a big part of life that most people took for granted. As a child, people assured me that my dreams of having a husband and family of my own would be easily attainable when I grew up. Now that I was actually a grown-up, it seemed like someone had suddenly changed the rules. I was still a nice person, wasn't I? I was a good person with a lot to offer. Perhaps I wasn't one of those perfect beauties on TV or in movies, but I had my own type of beauty, didn't I? Why couldn't anybody see this? Why couldn't anybody get past my disability?

When I was twenty-three, my parents put me into a home for people with physical and mental disabilities for "parent relief" while they went on their annual two-week vacation. There, I began having a relationship with one of the male attendants. He pursued me, kissed me, and told me I was beautiful and desirable. After I came home, we started dating. Finally, I thought I had found a man who liked me "in that way" and knew I had the same feelings and desires as any other woman. Finally, I could have a romantic relationship with a man just like any other woman. I was in love with him, or thought I was. But I never fooled myself into believing that he loved me. Even so, when he broke up with me to marry another disabled woman, it hurt like hell. Later on, I realized that what hurt most was the fear that I'd never find anyone else, that this man was my last chance at happiness.

At twenty-nine, I was resigned that I would die an old maid, a virgin forever, without a mate. If that's how things were going to be, then so be it. I had tried my best. Then something happened that changed my life. A friend of mine talked me into purchasing a computer and a modem, and showed me how to access a bulletin board system to communicate with people. From then on, I spent up to three hours a day in online chat rooms with total strangers talking about just about anything and everything.

One day, I logged on and began chatting with this guy named Rob. He seemed sweet and funny. We liked each other almost instantly. We chatted for hours and found that we had many things in common. Even so, I didn't feel comfortable enough at first to tell him that I had cerebral palsy. I was afraid of how he might react— I couldn't face another rejection!

Rob kept asking if he could meet me. When he told me he thought he was falling in love with me, I felt I had to break my silence. Amazingly, Rob didn't care about my disability. He still thought I was a wonderful person and wanted to meet me.

My family and friends thought I was nuts to go meet a guy I'd only chatted with for a month on the Internet. But I didn't care. I was confident that Rob would be just as he had seemed in the chat rooms. I was right! When we met, it was as if we had known each other all of our lives. We started dating and soon fell in love. Neither of us could have been happier. It was as if we had been made especially for each other.

We've been married for seven years and live happily in downtown Toronto. Finding Rob has taught me that if you want something badly enough, one day you just might get it. Just never give up hope or be afraid to take chances.

~

ANNE ABBOTT *is a freelance writer whose articles have appeared in such periodicals as* Communicating Together *and the magazine* abilities. *She is also a graphic artist whose paintings and handmade note cards are frequently displayed at Show Gallery in Toronto, Canada. Having painted since a child, Anne has found, through trial and error, that using her index finger as a paintbrush/pallet knife works best for her. A person who is nonspeaking herself, Anne is president pro term of Speaking Differently, an organization for people with communication disabilities. Anne lives with her husband, Rob, and cat, Dandylion, in the heart of downtown Toronto.*

5

EDUCATION ABOUT DISABILITY

HONESTY, THE BEST POLICY

Donna M. Laird

Is HONESTY ALWAYS the best policy? As a child with a physical
disability and then as a parent, my answer is "Yes, always!" Honesty is crucial for dealing with a child's disability and is fundamental to positive outcomes. While some may argue a child is better off
kept in the dark, it is just too hard to conceal the truth when, in our
highly technological society, access to information regarding a child's
disease or disability is as close as the touch of a button. More important, if your child comes to you wanting answers or you can see that
she is craving some insight into what is happening to her, as a loving parent, what are you to do? Several events in my life have convinced me that, along with a positive attitude, honesty is the best
policy—always.

From about the age of five, I had a feeling that I was different
from my brother and sister. I was always falling over and was never
able to keep up with them athletically. When I was eleven, my teachers advised my parents of my numerous falls and problems climbing
stairs. This led to accusations of seeking attention by my father and
being forced to get up off the floor in the conventional manner—
with the aid of a leather strap and verbal abuse. Later discussions
with my younger sister revealed how helpless and sad she felt as she
peeped around the corner and witnessed my torment.

My father did come to realize that there was a problem, and I was taken to the local physician. With an air of arrogance and viewing my mum as just another neurotic mother fussing over her child, the physician diagnosed elongated ligaments that were allowing my knees to give way and cause my falls. He sent me to a physiotherapist to do some exercises to strengthen my legs. After observing my attempts at climbing stairs and charting my muscle strength, the therapist sent me straight back to the physician, expressing her concerns and demanding further investigation.

We were referred to a neurologist in Sydney. He admitted me to a hospital for a battery of tests, including muscle biopsies on both my arm and leg. It was all very troubling to me because I thought the problem was just with my legs. Never, at any time, was I told the purpose of each test or procedure. A little reassurance and explanation would have gone a long way to ease my fears. These encounters left me with a lack of confidence, fear, and helplessness with the medical profession. It wasn't until I was much older and more informed that I regained more confidence and felt more empowered.

The test results were never really explained to my parents either. The neurologist told them that I had a muscle disease and that I would have to just go home and make the best of it. I was only told I had weak muscles—a truly inept explanation for a terrified child.

A move closer to family and superior medical facilities led us to a new physician. After reviewing the medical reports about me, he finally made a specific diagnosis of a neuromuscular disease called limb-girdle muscular dystrophy. But, I only found out about my diagnosis by overhearing a conversation between my parents and an uncle. It was a truly frightening experience because I absorbed totally misleading and out of context information—"it was a boy's disease and they usually died while still teenagers." I could only share the terrible news of a life-threatening disease with my close friend at school.

After my parents became involved in the local Muscular Dystrophy Association, I was able to get some information from the literature I would find around the house. Feeling very sorry for myself, I went through the "why me" stage and then moved on to blaming my parents and the world in general. It was a truly difficult time. It would have been so much easier for me if I had been informed of my condition and my various options—or if I felt I could approach my parents with my fears.

At age sixteen, I was finally convinced to use a wheelchair and sent away to a Rehabilitation Centre. I was trained for employment and underwent physical and occupational therapy as well as counseling. I experienced all sorts of new adventures and had heaps of laughs while learning just how lucky I was compared to some of the other patients. Knowing these other patients gave me the incentive to make the most of what I still had and to look for the positive in every situation.

Out in the real world, away from the Rehabilitation Centre, all sorts of people have touched my life, and I have found that having positive people around helps keep me positive. I have learned to avoid negative types like the social worker who broke down and sobbed while visiting me when I was a patient in an Intensive Care Unit and on a ventilator. Or, the nurse who blatantly asked how I could possibly deal with my condition as she would just want to die—not very comforting or professional. It is vitally important to surround your child with positive and happy people whenever possible.

Not to be forgotten are the siblings of the child with a disability. Their feelings can be overshadowed by the needs of the special child, and they can be called upon to perform tasks that ordinarily wouldn't be expected of them. As a result, they can feel neglected, inferior, and used. It is important that the avenues of communication are always open for them to discuss their fears and frustrations just as they are for the child with a disability. They may have questions regarding whether they too will contract the disease or need to be on the lookout for symptoms. When there is a genetic element involved with a disease, they may wish to be tested because of their concerns about passing the disease on to their children.

In conclusion, my advice to parents is to listen to your children and actually hear what they are saying. Be open and honest with your children in all aspects of their lives, from the most trivial questions to the major ones. As a parent I have adopted a policy of honesty right from the start with my son. He knows he can ask me any question about any topic without me being judgmental, and he can rely on an honest answer. Of course, knowing my own child influences the context in which the issue is addressed, as well as the extent of the information provided.

When your children know that you are approachable and are confident about your honesty, they will come to you rather than seek out answers from other venues that may not address the issue appropriately. In contrast to health professionals, teachers, family members, and friends who may disguise or misrepresent the facts, parents can highlight the positive and downgrade the negative while still retaining their honesty.

Ultimately, I believe a child with a disability should be treated as any other child. They are entitled to at least that much. Remain honest and open with all your children. If you make mistakes along the way, you can be reassured that you have been honest with the best intentions. After all, parents are human—and entitled to make mistakes.

~

DONNA LAIRD *lives in the coastal city of Newcastle, Australia, with her ten-year-old son, Sam. During her forty-one years, she has had numerous roles. Most important, she is a mother to a perfectly healthy, quite charming, and loving son. She is also a daughter, sister, aunt, friend, confidante, student, patient, client, divorcee, and sufferer of a neuromuscular disease, limb-girdle muscular dystrophy. Donna has been employed in several clerical/medical positions and is currently studying for a B.A. with a major in sociology.*

Her medical condition, with muscle weakness affecting all four limbs, torso, and lung capacity, has reached a stage requiring the permanent use of an electric wheelchair and hoist for transfers. As for the future, her main goals are to enjoy each day as it comes and to see her son grow into a happy, healthy, loved, and respected adult.

NO SECRETS: A KID IS A KID

Tracy Wright

Two things that my parents should have known while I was growing up are the importance of treating me like any other kid in the family and how to talk openly about disabilities. If they had done that, I would not have spent so much time worrying that it was my fault that I was being treated differently. It also would have helped me to know that I was smart and could learn things, just in a different way. If people had talked about my disability, I don't think I would have felt as embarrassed about it and I would not have apologized for it as much.

I want to tell parents of young children with disabilities that it is important to include their children with disabilities in every area of life—because they are going to grow up someday and it will help them be more self-confident. People with disabilities should be prepared to live their lives when they grow up, just like everyone else.

When I was young, I went to a special education wing in my school. We were kept away from the regular population. It made it hard to know how to make friends and build relationships with people. As a kid, I felt that I was special in a way that is not really special at all. This didn't prepare me for the things that were going to be expected of me outside of the special education wing. I didn't learn the right things for future real-life experiences. There were no expectations for us to learn responsibility, respect for yourself and others, and how to introduce yourself and make friends.

My advice is to expose your kids to all the opportunities that you expose any other kid to. Maybe I don't read as well, but let me go to the library with other kids and teach me the same responsibilities. Maybe I need support to fill out and get a library card or to take the library book back. But teach me how to ask for support and that I have the responsibility to ask for the support I need. Encourage teachers to include me in all parts of the lessons each school day, so I get exposed to new ideas—even though I might not understand everything in the traditional way of learning.

I can remember my cousins all having responsibilities after a big family gathering and giving me a hard time about not having to do anything. This just made me feel different, again. I wanted to help and feel needed, too. Family responsibility is just as important as outside responsibility, and family expectations are important. If you are not given responsibility and nothing is expected of you in your family, how can you ever be able to do it in other places? Give your children with disabilities responsibilities and consequences—just like any other child.

If I would have been treated the same as other kids in the family and we talked about my disability, it would have helped me to think about my future. No one ever asked me, like they asked other kids, "What do you want to be when you grow up?" My family members were afraid to talk about this because no one knew what my future could be. They were so focused on the daily struggles; it was too much to think about the future.

Kids with disabilities are going to grow up. They need to think about a future and plan like anybody else. If they are not talked to about these issues, it is going to be that much harder to make decisions. So, if we had been more open about my disability, maybe we could have talked about my future. Then, when I had to make these decisions, it would have been easier. We also might have looked for more options, rather than just where the "special" people went to live.

It is important to help children understand that they have a disability. But the disability is only part of who they are, not all of who they are. I would never want a child to feel embarrassed or ashamed about his or her disability or try to hide it. It's all part of learning to be proud of all of who you are. If you are taught to understand your disability, then you can help other people be comfortable with your disability as well. It does not have to be the focus of why people are interested in being your friend. But, it can be a part of getting to know you as a person—because your disability is a part of you.

Parents can help by learning about the disability and the different forms of the disability. Then they can share what they have learned with all members of the family. This would be good because all the children are growing up and have questions. The disability would not be a secret that no one talked about in their daily life. Of course, it should not be the only focus of family discussions. But, it is something that the family is going through together and will always be there.

Remember, when you get caught up in the whole disability thing, enjoy all your children. Even try to enjoy the struggles—it will make you a better person. Disability does not have to be this bad thing that people cannot get past to enjoy and live life. You just might have to go about it in a little different way.

≈

TRACY WRIGHT *is thirty-three years old and lives in Rockville, Maryland, with her one-year-old son, Robert, and her service dog, Butler. Tracy works for The Arc of Maryland on several advocacy projects. She is also very active in volunteer work. She is the cochair of People On the Go of Maryland and serves on local and state committees.*

Tracy is currently pursuing her bachelor's degree in social work. Recently, she received her associate's degree.

Tracy started in advocacy work when she graduated from Partners in Policymaking, a leadership training program. She has become well respected in the disability community and is turned to for ideas and planning for the future. Tracy is very proud of obtaining a housing voucher and moving from a segregated apartment building to a typical community apartment complex. Robert and Butler are very much a part of her successful advocacy efforts.

TWICE EXCEPTIONAL

Kassiane A. Sibley

M ANY TIMES PARENTS SUSPECT that their child is a genius. Others fear that their offspring might have a hidden or not-yet-identified disability or difference. Usually neither is the case. The majority of kids are, by definition, average. In our society, no one seems to want to be "average." The word is almost seen as an insult. But it is not. There is no shame in being wired like the majority.

Sometimes the parents are right, and their child does display unusual intellectual promise. And sometimes, the children of these parents do display a disability. Neither one of these situations is uncommon, nor is it hard to find other families who deal with similar issues. It is less commonplace and less well known when the parents are right on both counts: yes, their child is intellectually gifted, and yes, their child has a disability. When this is the case, the child is said to be twice exceptional.

A person who is twice exceptional has both a disability and intellectual gifts. This needs to be contrasted with savant syndrome, in which the person has one or two very, very strong areas of achievement, but otherwise functions on a much lower-than-average level. Children and adults who are twice exceptional have a full-scale intelligence quotient in the gifted range. Like all people, these students have strengths and weaknesses, but overall the twice exceptional learner is very intelligent.

Differences that can accompany giftedness include, but are not limited to, learning disabilities such as dyslexia and dyscalculia, attention deficit disorders, physical differences of all types, health difficulties, autistic spectrum conditions, emotional or behavioral disorders, and almost any other condition that exists in the human condition. Depending on the disability and how pronounced it is, the giftedness or the difference may be noticed first.

A twice exceptional child will also be a twice exceptional learner, student, and adult. All of these areas present their own unique challenges. I know this because I fall into this category: I am a college student with an autistic spectrum condition and intelligence in the genius range. Because I did not have a pronounced speech delay or an obvious lack of social drive, my giftedness was pointed out well before my autism. I learned to read before I was three, which is actually an indicator of hyperlexia, a condition that occurs frequently in people on the autistic spectrum, but it was seen as proof of my superior intellect.

My school years in a typical classroom were rough. Since all the adults assumed it was because I was bored, I was tested for the gifted school. I got in, but I had an even harder time in that program. By high school, I had fallen completely apart, but I did not get an answer as to why until about three months before graduation.

Back when I was a kid, twice exceptionality was not really recognized. Smart kids did not have attention deficit, autism, bipolar disorder, or any other sort of hidden disability. By this time, it was recognized that those with physical differences can have superior intelligence. Students like me—those who were obviously bright but could not make friends or get their schoolwork done consistently—were labeled with far more harmful words than the ones used to describe our differences. Before being autistic, I was considered lazy, spoiled, unmotivated, bratty, and just plain strange. Those terms caused far more pain than any diagnosis possibly could.

Words like *lazy* and *unmotivated* hurt the twice exceptional learner in more than one way. First, they are very harsh terms to apply to any child. Second, ignoring the real issue of a hidden difference prevents the person from getting the help he or she needs to achieve his or her full potential. In addition, words like *lazy* can become a self-fulfilling prophecy. There is no reason for the child to continue working twice as hard as everyone else if he is going to be considered lazy for his efforts, so he may become lazy or unmotivated. If a disability is not identified and the affected child begins to fail, it can set that child up for a cycle of failures that is harder and harder to reverse as time goes on. Not only that, if a child has to come up with his own strategies for dealing with his difference, the strategies may be the type that irritate adults, thereby getting the child in trouble and making him feel even more like a failure than he already does.

Now that we have established that being considered to have a disability is less harmful than being considered all sorts of other adjectives, it is time to discuss accommodations. These can be hard to secure for a person who is twice exceptional, especially in school, because the student might perform at an average or even above-average level without help. There are two problems with denying help on this basis. First, the learner is probably working much harder than she should have to just to keep up. Second, if one is significantly above the norm, no one is going to be satisfied with typical work and the student is probably very frustrated with herself.

Now, I am covering my ears because I can hear everyone shouting at the book, "But you said there is no shame in being average!" You're right, I did say that. There is no shame at all in being average, if you yourself are an average person. However, everyone has a personal average and the individual's performance should be in that range. The gifted student's personal intellectual average is well above that of her typical peers. The idea of education is not to let all students achieve mediocrity—the goal is full potential.

Disability should not get in the way, like average can; *disability* is not a dirty word.

Sometimes, educators feel that if a student is doing very well with accommodations, it is time to remove them. Just recently an instructor of mine resisted allowing my accommodations. Because of sensory sensitivities, I receive all tests on green paper and I am allowed to put a laminated piece of paper under my hand to write, wear earplugs as needed, and wear dark glasses—all with no questions asked. I tend to be the first person done with tests, and I get top grades. Because of this, my instructor commented that she did not think my earplugs and green paper were really necessary. I am in college and could tell her that school is not set up for people like me, and that, given my intelligence, I should be getting As. I could also tell her that my earplugs certainly did not afford an unfair advantage, that my accommodations merely make the environment tolerable, not ideal, and that the green paper and laminate sheet had at least as much benefit for her as they did for me, as they rendered my penmanship legible. A child is not likely to be able to talk like this to a teacher. That is why educators and parents need to know that sometimes even smart kids need some things to be done differently.

Twice exceptional individuals are one of the most under-identified groups. We have the intellectual ability to make a big difference, but we can only achieve our full potential if we are given supports to help us through our weak areas. In some ways being twice exceptional is harder than being either gifted or having a disability, and it is definitely harder than being average. But, it is who I was born to be. I would not trade in my difficulties for anything, because there are good points, too—and without the struggles and the ease together, I would not be me.

~

KASSIANE SIBLEY *is a special education major from central Illinois. Quite by accident, she discovered that she has high-functioning autism while in her senior year of high school. In addition to writing about living on the autistic spectrum, she enjoys tumbling and trampoline, spending time with other autistic people, attending autism conferences, and hanging out with her very special group of friends. Kassiane has spoken publicly about autism on several occasions and refers to herself as autistic, not as a person with autism. Kassiane lives with two parents, her stepbrother, and three dogs of various sizes. Her long-term goals include starting a tumbling program for children with special needs, teaching an all autistic and Asperger's class, and publishing a book about her experiences.*

DOES YOUR CHILD HAVE EPILEPSY? SO DO I!

John G. Miers

NOTHING UPSETS PARENTS MORE than learning that one of their children has a health-related problem. Parents are nurturing and protective and want nothing but the best for their children.

When confronted by an illness in one of their children, parents have a wide range of responses, from cautious and concerned to profound fear. This is even more likely if the problem is due to something that they don't really understand, such as epilepsy. Parents can become overprotective when their child with epilepsy wants to try a new activity—like swimming or riding a bicycle—if the parent believes that there could be a real danger involved in the activity.

Having a seizure can change a child's life in dramatic ways and set a child apart from friends and siblings. A child with epilepsy can become confused when he or she doesn't understand about his or her own condition. Even when they are having seizures regularly, some children with epilepsy have never actually seen a person having a seizure. Or, they don't understand what happens when they themselves have one. It can be even more confusing when the only consistent parental message seems to be that he or she isn't "allowed" to do many things that friends and siblings can do. Sometimes, a child with epilepsy may be teased or believe that this will be the case.

In addition, having epilepsy usually means multiple medical tests, many doctor visits, and possibly medications.

I've been there, too. When I was a baby, I had several seizures. The doctor reassured my parents that I would be fine. But, when I was twelve, I had another seizure. My mother, being a nurse, took me to a pediatric neurologist, who again reassured us that I would be all right—"if it didn't happen again." It did happen again. My seizures became gradually more frequent. First I was having seizures every six months, then every three months, and, by the time I was in college, monthly. My epilepsy became harder to live with, but I got used to it—sort of. While I had the good fortune of never being teased, I still did not feel quite whole. My seizures are still not controlled, but I have an understanding and helpful family.

What advice can I give about speaking with your child about epilepsy? First and foremost, parents and children may be reassured by the old saying that God doesn't make junk. Every single person is a unique combination of strengths and weaknesses. It is also important for everyone involved, both children and parents, to take "ownership" of the disorder. This means being aware and concerned in order to be on top of the situation.

Be frank and honest about what is going on, what needs to be done, and what should not be done. Doing this can be difficult and perplexing because parents want to urge their children to do as much as they can, while being aware of specific activities that may pose a threat. Parents and children need to be cautious but not overwhelmed with fear. Often the physician or health practitioner working with your child can help in setting appropriate limits.

Parents want their child to be healed. Children want to be healed, too. In fact, for many people, their seizures are controlled through medication, surgery, or special diets, or just over time. While some people do seem to grow out of their seizures, others seem to grow into them. For children and parents, as well as for physicians, the uncertainty of possible outcomes is challenging.

I remember when I was a camp counselor for children with seizures. It was our first night in the cabin. There were about a dozen boys, ages six, seven, and eight, and three counselors. After dinner, we were having "Circle Time," talking about the events of the day and our plans for tomorrow. I then brought up some specific questions: "What is a seizure?" "What does a seizure look like?" "What should you do when someone has a seizure?" Nobody knew the answers. Most of the younger boys had never seen anyone having a seizure.

Suddenly, almost on cue, one boy had a seizure. I held him and protected him and sent the assistant counselor for the nurse. The nurse arrived promptly and took him to her office. We then talked about the seizure in the group: what it was, what to do, and what not to do. They learned a lot that night. One child explained how upset he was about his parents wanting him to have a Medic Alert bracelet. When I showed him mine, he felt better.

As parents, what can we do in order to help others live with their seizures? What can we tell our children, their friends, their siblings, their teachers, and other adults? What about the parents of their friends? Most of all, we need to tell them that it is OK for our children to play together. We can explain that a child may have a seizure some time and show them how to handle a child with a seizure. With such information, there will be far less fear.

To educate ourselves, our children, and others in the community, we need to know the latest information from nonprofit organizations such as the Epilepsy Foundation (epilepsyfoundation.org), government agencies like the National Institute of Neurological Disorders and Stroke (ninds.nih.gov), and our child's physician. There are also support groups, for both individuals with epilepsy and parents, that can help us learn.

We also need to ensure that our children know about their epilepsy, including what they can and cannot do, both now and in the future. It is important to be optimistic; it helps to see the glass as half-filled, not half-empty. It is important to look to the future and to be hopeful. The challenges that we face will change over time, requiring both parents and children to keep abreast of the emerging issues in epilepsy diagnosis and treatment.

Knowledge and perseverance are essential, as well as a positive, optimistic attitude. Good luck!

~

JOHN MIERS *is employed by a federal agency as director of its Office of Diversity and Employee Advocacy Programs, having worked in the government since he earned his master's degree.*

In disability activities, he is on his agency's disability committee and serves as a commissioner in the County Commission for People with Disabilities. He has been a counselor at a camp for children with epilepsy. He is also active in the Episcopal Church, at the local, diocese, and national levels and enjoys being a member of the singing and bell choirs in his church. John serves on the board for a halfway house for persons recovering from mental illness and has received an award for community service. He has worked in rebuilding a burned church in South Carolina and with the chaplain of a local hospital.

Married, with three grown daughters and a grandson, John enjoys gardening.

LEARNING WAS ALWAYS HARD FOR ME

Damaris A. Mills

I AM A FIFTY-THREE-YEAR-OLD with severe attention deficit hyperactivity disorder (ADHD), dyslexia, and dyscalculia (a math deficit).

Ever since I was a small child, I was curious and liked learning, but it was always very hard for me. My favorite learning times in school were when the teacher showed films and filmstrips. We did not know until years later that I was a visual learner.

By the time I was in fourth grade, I was having a lot of trouble in math. In fact, there was a group of about five or six of us who had to stay after school three or four times a week, because we did so poorly with our studies. We were sort of like those kids in that movie *The Breakfast Club*, only our little club didn't just meet on one Saturday morning. We had to work on the math that we couldn't grasp in class, or English, because we couldn't keep our verbs and conjunctions straight, or American History, because we were distracted in class or just couldn't memorize all those dates and places. I also always had trouble with book reports—because I could never read fast enough to finish a whole book, because I would get stuck on words and whole sentences, and because I couldn't remember all of the important details. At least my penmanship and spelling were pretty good, but that did not prevent me from staying back.

But being in that "stay-after-school" group was so humiliating. First of all, I was the only girl in the group, so that alone was ammunition for teasing. Then, most of the boys in the group were known troublemakers, so having to stay after school with these guys left a certain stigma. As it was, having to stay after school in the first place usually felt like a punitive measure, no matter what the reason. But I was not a bad kid; I just had trouble with my schoolwork. Looking back on it now, I don't think my club mates were bad either. Probably, all of us were victims of some sort of learning disabilities. But back then in the 1950s and early 1960s, learning disabilities were unheard of.

I was constantly being put down by my teacher and scolded by my mother. Many days, I wished I could make myself invisible so the teacher wouldn't call on me when I didn't know the answers— but she did. Then when I did know the answers and raised my hand, the teacher wouldn't call on me. Needless to say, my self-esteem was practically nonexistent. I even tried hiding my report card from my mother once because it consisted mostly of Ds. But moms always have a way of finding stuff out. When she found that card, boy did she read me the riot act! To this day, I still don't know how the heck she found my hiding place.

Since my mom knew I had to stay after school so much because of my schoolwork, I wish she had done a more thorough investigation as to why I was having so much trouble. Instead, she just believed the teacher who was saying that I was just lazy and not trying. It's not right that a kid should be punished just because she's having trouble learning. But like I said before, people were not really aware of learning disabilities back then, so parents had to rely on what the teachers told them.

Patience, understanding, and compassion are needed when a child is having difficulty with learning. Most of all, a child needs to be listened to. Every time I tried to tell my mom about my troubles in school, she would tell me, "Well, the teacher got her education, now you have to get yours." Even though I hated to hear those words, I appreciate them and my mom for saying them, because they became so ingrained in my brain that I became obsessed about getting my education. However, teachers, just because they are teachers, are not always right. That's why it is important for us to listen to our children, so they won't be afraid to come to us about such things.

Another major problem that I had as a child was cleaning my room. Clutter happened so quickly. I was so easily distracted. When I'd be working on one thing, I would get sidetracked and go to something else, leaving whatever I had first been working on. By the time my mom would tell me to clean my room, at least once a week, I never knew where to begin. I could spend a whole day in that room just trying to figure out how to begin.

It would have been much easier for me if my mom had assigned me one task at a time in my room. Such as, "First change your bedding, Damaris." Then, "Now pick up your dirty laundry." Next, "Now clean off your desk," and so on and so on. I still have trouble today when I let my room get out of hand. But even now, I have people who work with me (coaches) to give me guidance.

When my sons were in elementary and middle school, I needed to take one son to a neurologist on the recommendation of his teacher. It turned out that both of us had mild forms of Tourette syndrome and severe ADHD. Later, we found out that my other son had the same conditions. So, both the boys and I were tested and ADHD was confirmed. However, it was not determined through testing that we were dyslexic. This was not discovered until both my boys were out of school and grown and I went to Landmark College—a college specifically for students with ADHD, dyslexia, and other specific learning disabilities. My own dyslexia was discovered when I was there, and it was later realized that my sons were dyslexic, too.

If you have your child tested, make sure they are tested for everything. Ask prospective testers if they test for dyslexia and other learning disabilities, in addition to ADHD. Testing is usually done by psychologists. Additional information about learning disabilities/differences can be found on a great Internet website, LD OnLine (ldonline.com). The site is jam-packed with information about different kinds of learning disabilities; ways to find help; a kid's section where they can do fun, educational things; and much, much more.

Among the many items at LD OnLine is a section called "First Person Essays." I graduated from Landmark College in December 2002. While I was there, I had this wonderful psychology professor who wrote a "First Person Essay." In the essay, one of the things he spoke about was the way he allows his students to use their various intelligences to help them to understand the concepts he is teaching. For example, when I was in his class, we were learning about the parts of the brain. He always gave us additional information sources such as various website links. In this case, I went to a kid's science Web link that had great pictures and broken-down details of the brain. From this source, I was able to construct a large brain out of poster board and construction paper. By doing this, it was easier for me to memorize the parts of the brain and details, because I am a visual, hands-on learner.

After finding out about my own learning differences and then my children's, and then discovering there are many other successful—and famous—people with some of the same problems, I now feel like I can do anything I put my mind to.

From sharing a bit about myself and some informational sources, hopefully, your child won't have to become my age before he or she can get the kind of help that is needed.

~

HAVING A LEARNING DIFFERENCE *and other embarrassing disabilities was devastating to Damaris Mills: "I strayed down many dan-*

gerous paths because I felt so bad about myself. For years, I felt stupid and thought I was retarded and nobody would tell me."

Damaris was an unwed teen mother, became a hippie, used drugs and alcohol, and was a confused and terrified person for many years. Now, she has been blessed in finding the right place to "learn how to learn." She has a second chance in life and is an example to her children and eight grandchildren.

Damaris has been clean and sober for a few years now. She is training to become a reading tutor to help others with dyslexia—with compassion and understanding because she has been there. She is also writing a book about her journey while working a home-based catalog business. Damaris hopes to attend Smith College in 2005.

PLEASE DON'T BE PUT OFF BY YOUR DOCTOR

Evelyn Toseland

I WAS BORN IN 1954. I now know that I have severe allergies, particularly to nuts, eggs, feathers, wool, dust, pollen, and molds, as well as moderate to severe asthma, combined with irreparable lung damage resulting from the lack of proper treatment I received as a child. The nut allergy is severe enough to be classed as life-threatening and is similar to that diagnosed in some young children nowadays.

My asthma and allergies are classified as a disability because they have a severe impact on what I can and cannot do. Mine is an "invisible" disability. I admit I have sometimes envied people with more obvious disabilities—people with invisible disabilities get no concessions at all.

I grew up in Leeds, an industrial town in northern England, with thick, acidic coal-smog occurring at least once during each of my first ten winters, until the Clean Air Act cut down on pollution. Leeds is infamous for its cold, damp weather.

I had all the usual childhood ailments but with asthma always "on top." When I had the flu, I had asthma. When I had measles, chickenpox, and mumps, I had asthma. When I got cold playing sports at school or wet in the constant Leeds rain, I had asthma. Whenever I had a cold, I ended up with at least a day off from school with asthma.

Usually I slept propped up in my bed with three or more feather pillows. Because I often felt cold, a side effect of asthma, I had a thick feather quilt and fluffy woolen blankets on my bed. Many nights I would struggle into my parents' room and whisper ". . . can't breathe. . . ." Then, my mother (always my mother, as Daddy worked long, demanding hours as an engineer) would get up with me, never complaining. We developed a routine: she would settle me on the couch in our living room, complete with my feather quilt, my pillows, and a cup of tea. I would sit wheezing away the rest of the night and get catnaps, waking with my chest hurting, coughing and sneezing, my nose completely stuffed up, and severe postnasal drip. My eyes would fill with mucus and the skin around them would puff up—I could barely see. My mother and I used to call this effect "piggy eyes." I later learned it was a symptom of an allergic reaction. I spent a lot of my childhood with piggy eyes.

After a night of asthma, I was too tired to go to school. Once the worst of the asthma was over, I got dressed, sat around, without my quilt or pillows, and watched daytime TV or read—and slowly recovered. I read a lot and essentially educated myself.

One of my sisters and my mother loved peanuts. They used to roast them and then shell off the papery skins on our kitchen table. The smell of peanuts always bothered me, and I tended to avoid going near them. We had no suspicion that I was sensitive to nuts (allergies were unheard of—all food was good food) till one day at a cousin's birthday party. Aunt Elsie had made a beautiful, rich, chocolate birthday cake with creamy chocolate and hazelnut icing. I got sick. Boy—did I get sick! Overexcitement was mentioned, but we did wonder about nuts from then on.

To visit Aunt Linde's farm, we would go by train and come back by car. My father used to wonder why I always got carsickness on the way back. But it is human nature to look for explanations, even if they are wrong. We decided it was "motion sickness" or "overexcitement." I loved going to the farm. I was able to run around and play more like my sisters and cousins, although still puffing a little—until we had tea and Aunt Linde's cakes, which usually included nuts.

Asthma is now recognized as provoked by allergic responses. In those days in the United Kingdom, the medical profession did not know about such things as allergies. Asthma was rare and generally only diagnosed in life-threatening cases. Otherwise, it was called "wheezy bronchitis" and treated with cough syrup. The only person I knew of who was diagnosed as asthmatic was the mother of a school friend. She was very ill indeed and spent a good deal of her life in an iron lung at a hospital. Growing up imagining a future in an iron lung was frightening.

Our family physician was less than helpful. Because he would not come out to the house at night, he never saw me in the throes of a real attack. By the time I was about eight, my mother and I had figured out that I got asthma after every physical education class at school. At our regular visits to the doctor, our requests for a note for the physical education teacher were met with the response, "Well, she is a little tubby, isn't she? She needs to run about and lose some weight. Then she wouldn't get wheezy."

There was no way I could "run about." I plodded, slowly. The penalty for any running was a severe "soot-fall," as we called it, and either a disgusting wet cough like that of a heavy smoker, to which the usual response was "Cough it up, love, it might be a gold watch!" Or, more often the response was a dry, gasping cough where there did not seem to be enough air getting into my lungs to bring up a digital watch battery, never mind a gold watch.

My father, disillusioned with orthodox medicine, tried dosing me with homeopathic medicines. These helped, but certainly did not heal. My uncle studied naturopathy and prescribed parsley tea and no milk. It did not help, but I had a miserable year's trial of his theory and now hate parsley with a vengeance!

When I was eleven, my mother decided my constantly stuffed-up nose must be due to polyps in the nose. She insisted that I see a specialist. After deciding that I had no polyps, the specialist suggested "allergy tests"—something our family doctor had never mentioned and we had never heard of. I had a series of skin-prick tests (scratch tests with a needle dipped into essences; if you are allergic to the substance, the area scratched becomes swollen and itchy). When my lumps came up several centimeters across, I was diagnosed as having strong allergic reactions to many household substances—household dust, feathers, wool, grass and tree pollens, and, not surprisingly, nuts. The feather pillows and wool blankets I had been wrapped up in all those long, gasping nights had prolonged the agony.

Although my mother never said a word about the bedding, I suddenly found new pillows and different blankets on my bed. The new pillows and different blankets were a huge improvement. Once we removed the feathers and woolen blankets from my bedroom, I slept better. And, I stopped eating Aunt Linde's and Aunt Elsie's cakes. My school attendance improved and I had an almost normal lifestyle, with only occasional bouts of asthma—when I got cold and wet playing hockey or walking home from school.

I still pay for the early years. Having asthma causes me difficulties at work and limits my recreation. It affects, and will probably shorten, my whole life. The nut allergy means I have to avoid certain shops. It causes me some difficulties when traveling, and we very rarely eat out.

I don't blame my parents. They did their best with the information they had. In working-class Leeds at that time, one did not question the doctor's judgment, even if one thought him a fool as they did, nor did one change doctors. My parents did experiment with alternatives as much as they could afford, within a limited budget. Research papers and medical journals were not available to the public as they are now.

My message to parents? If your child has an odd symptom, find out more. If there is sensitivity or any kind of pattern, follow it up.

Get on the Internet and read all the research. Question your doctor, or ask another. You are not being a fussy parent. Do it before it's too late. You could save your child, and yourself, a lot of grief.

~

EVELYN TOSELAND *lives in Bristol, England, which is warmer and a little drier than Leeds. She is married with three children and two grandchildren. Her children also have allergy problems and relatively mild asthma. Her husband, who has a doctorate in theology and is registered blind, researches New Testament theology.*

Evelyn worked in the civil service and then managed a series of delicatessen counters until a close encounter with peanut oil drove her out of the retail trade and into a complete career change. She discovered the Internet with delight soon after it became available to the public in 1993 and now works as a Web designer for a provincial university. Until a recent spate of ill health, she was chair of her staff union, with particular interest in disability issues.

LISTENING IS THE KEY

Ross Mattingly

I'VE HAD A LOT OF GROWING PAINS since I've faced the challenges of living with cerebral palsy and a learning disability every day of my life. I'm thankful that I have caring parents who provided for my needs. But, I wish they had tried to learn more about cerebral palsy and how it affects people. I'll admit that can be a difficult task because cerebral palsy affects everyone differently. Just the same, I do wish my parents better understood my own strengths and weaknesses. Mostly, I wish they had listened to my thoughts and feelings more.

Sometimes, it's easy to tell that individuals with cerebral palsy have a disability because the individual's impairments in motor skills or speech can be seen or heard. Some types of cerebral palsy are less noticeable. The main outward sign that shows I have a disability is that I walk with a limp. And, like some people with cerebral palsy, I'm slow at learning some things.

Since the signs of my cerebral palsy weren't visible, I believe, at times, my parents may not have considered how my disability was affecting me. Sometimes, they would push me beyond my limits. I remember as a kid, Dad would ask me to help him work on a car. Maybe he was trying to teach me about automobiles, but I had trouble kneeling beside a car because my left leg is a half-inch shorter than my right one. And, although I couldn't actually work on a car, my father expected me to walk up and down a hill to retrieve tools for him from his shed. As a result of my young age and my learning disability, this was a difficult task for me. It probably took me longer than most children to search for the tools he requested, and I also had a tough time telling the difference between a wrench and a socket of the same size. After a while, I learned to tell them apart by looking at the engraved numbers on the wrench and socket.

Not being able to do exactly what Dad requested troubled me. I wanted to make both my parents happy and proud of their only child. I wish Dad had understood that part of my brain was damaged. Since my brain damage caused me to have difficulty understanding things as easily and quickly as most children, I made more mistakes than Dad probably thought I should.

When I was in elementary school, I had to wear special shoes to help me walk. The left shoe was particularly painful—physically, as well as emotionally—for me to wear. It had a lift to compensate for my shorter leg as well as a brace attached to the shoe heel that came up to my kneecap. Wearing that brace was very painful because the piece that wrapped around my knee chafed my skin from constant rubbing. The shoes also had metal taps on them to prevent me from wearing my shoes out so quickly because I couldn't help dragging my left foot when I walked. But the sound those taps made on the floor as I walked seemed to annoy people, including my classmates and teachers. In fact, I was often punished for disturbing the class as I walked in and out of the room.

Unfortunately, the school bullies picked on me, presumably because they saw me as an easy target since I was small for my age and had cerebral palsy. They probably thought that they impressed their friends when they mistreated me since my disability prevented me from being able to protect myself. And, I wouldn't fight back anyway because my parents taught me that violence wouldn't solve anything. I also believed they bullied me because my unique shoes made me appear different.

Although I'm sure the teachers saw how some of my classmates mistreated me, they didn't do anything to stop my abuse. After enduring the agony of constantly being bullied at school for months, I finally found enough courage to try to tell my mother about it. But it seemed like both of my parents were more interested in watching the news than listening to me. This took place during the time of the Cold War and the Cuban missile crisis—that was why Mom and Dad intently watched the news. Being a young boy, I didn't understand why the news was important. To me, it seemed that my parents weren't interested in anything I said. I felt the only thing I could do was to bottle up my emotional pain inside myself. Silently, I cried myself to sleep many nights.

I blamed my torment mostly on my noisy, odd-looking shoes. One day, because of the frustration that had built up inside of me, I threw my left shoe with the brace in the trash. I knew I would be punished, but being spanked by my parents was better than having to go through the misery of wearing those shoes every day. Of course, my mother retrieved my shoe from the trash. After crying myself to sleep that night fearing what was going to happen to me, I wondered why no one had awakened me to go to school the next morning. I guess Mom finally realized that I actually was being mistreated because she told me that I was being transferred to another school.

That's why I believe it's important for parents to listen to their children, especially if they have disabilities. I'm aware that some children make up stories so that they won't have to do something they don't like to do. That may have been the reason my father and mother thought I was imagining my pain. I wish I had been able to share more of my feelings with my parents as I grew up because, like most children with disabilities, I had to face many challenges during my childhood.

Based on my own childhood experiences, I believe the most important element of parenting a child with a disability is communicating effectively with him or her. Parents should listen closely and with an open mind to whatever the child is saying—even if it's difficult for him or her to relay thoughts and feelings due to mental or physical disabilities. In my opinion, parents shouldn't assume that their child with a disability is imagining or inventing stories. Open and honest communication benefits both parents and children by establishing better understanding between them.

~

ROSS MATTINGLY *was born with cerebral palsy in Virginia in the late 1950s. He currently resides alone in a Georgia city. He has always been interested in music and enjoys playing the acoustic and electric guitar. Ross's father is one of his greatest musical influences because he entertained people with his singing and guitar playing ever since Ross can remember. Playing the guitar has always been therapeutic for Ross (especially when he was confined in a cast from his waist down as a teenager after leg surgery). The guitar provided an activity he could do in spite of his disability.*

He has always had great empathy for others with disabilities and wants to assist and encourage them. Hopefully, sharing some of the personal challenges he has faced as a man with cerebral palsy will improve the lives of other individuals with disabilities.

AS MUCH LOVE AS YOU CAN MUSTER

Lesley A. Jones

THANKS TO UNDIAGNOSED Asperger's syndrome (AS), I grew up in "Backwards Land." I walked funny and couldn't play sports well. I was chastised for, and embarrassed by, my strange gestures and habits. I was bullied by other children—and sometimes even by teachers! I couldn't write properly (dysgraphia); I often misunderstood what people were saying to me (central auditory processing disorder); and I sometimes had a hard time recognizing people (mild prosopagnosia). I was often criticized for choosing to spend my time with books rather than my peers. I was a bright child, but I couldn't get the help I needed—because I was bright. I floundered because, until I was an adult, I wasn't able to get the diagnosis that marked the beginning of my true self-understanding.

Today, life has really improved for the child with AS. But I still hear parents talk about many problems with their children, their children's teachers, and their children's peers. While I can't go back and change my childhood, by taking you on a tour of Backwards Land as I experienced it, maybe I can help you to understand more about your priceless child and how to help her or him navigate the often frustrating paths of Backwards Land with a little more grace.

As you well know, your child has a unique perspective on the world. You have a child who can see that the emperor has no clothes and doesn't hesitate to tell everyone. There are difficulties and hardships involved with raising (or being!) a child who really does march to the beat of a different drummer—a child with a neurology so different he sometimes seems to come from another planet, yet so similar to those around him that people are frequently puzzled when you tell them your child has special needs. But you know all too well that even though your child is amazingly skilled in certain areas, there are those gaps, those empty places—those disabilities that you and your child wrestle with every day.

I can't tell you how to raise your child. Even if I could, my answer would just be, "with as much love as you can muster." But I can tell you some of the things I would change about my own childhood. Hopefully, my insights will shine some light on your child's world. If I could turn back the clock and make some changes, here are things I'd try to make different.

I'd get a proper diagnosis. The pain you felt when your child was diagnosed with AS may have blinded you to the true gift of that diagnosis. Most parents are very upset to learn that their child has AS. But, stop to think about the difficulties of my labelless childhood and be grateful that someone has identified your child's problem and provided the means to help people understand and respect your child's needs. With the verification provided by an official label, you can fight to secure the proper individualized education plan (IEP) for your child and feel wholly justified in that battle. Everyone knows that a child with a disability needs accommodations! When you count your blessings, don't forget to count an accurate diagnosis for your child.

If I could change my childhood, adults would have focused more on the things I could do and spent less time punishing me for the things I couldn't do. I often hear parents say, "we refuse to use AS as an excuse," and I think that's good. However, expecting a child with AS to think, feel, and act like a child without AS is too much of a burden. Children need permission to be angry—as long as they learn not to lash out at others. Children need permission to find things difficult—as long as they never give up the fight to learn new things. Each child needs permission to be the child she or he is—not the child everyone wishes her or him to be.

Being lectured to and chastised all the time made me alternate between rage and withdrawal. I think it's easy to get caught up in a desire to help a child succeed and a frustration with their limitations—and end up pushing them too hard. I appreciate that my parents didn't give up on trying to help me succeed, but I wish they could have spent more time letting me know that they were proud of the things that I could do. I was a very sensitive child, and I wasn't very good at understanding that my parents loved me just by looking at their actions. I needed to hear the words, too. Your child can't guess that you love her or him—tell them, and do it often!

If I could go back in time and change things, the adults in my life would realize that I wasn't learning new social skills just by being exposed to lots of children every day. Children with AS don't "absorb" social rules the way other children do. I used to beg to be home-schooled instead of being thrown back in the "shark tank" of school. I understand now that my parents didn't have the time or resources to home-school me. But with a proper diagnosis, there should have been other options that would have exposed me to less peer abuse and more opportunities for personal and social growth. If your child complains of bullying, please take her or him seriously and do whatever you can to change the situation!

If I could change my past, I would have been allowed to use a typewriter for my schoolwork when I asked for it (third grade) instead of being pushed to complete mountains of schoolwork with insufficient motor skills. I wish I'd been tutored in handwriting by a therapist, but allowed to type my class work so that it would be legible. I would have had a much better chance of keeping up with my classmates and not had to suffer the dual insult of being punished for poor handwriting and, then, being punished for poor performance caused by my poor handwriting.

If I could rewrite my history, I would have been placed in gentler gym classes, designed to help less coordinated students, where I wouldn't have to suffer through kickball, basketball, or (shudder) dodgeball. I understand that sports are supposed to help children learn team spirit. But how much team spirit can a child learn who is constantly insulted for poor performance? After the team captains had chosen everyone for their teams except me, they would sometimes ask if they could just play with a team short one player—instead of having to take me on their team. That's no environment for a child to learn how to become a team player!

For sports, I wish I'd been placed with children with other mild physical disabilities. I could have learned more about accommodating others and caring about others' special needs. Because all players would have been more evenly matched in skills, no one would have batted an eye at my terrible clumsiness and inability to kick, throw, or catch a ball. If your child is treated like less than a person when it comes to sports, look for new options. You probably can't change the attitudes of those children your child has been playing with, but you may be able to get your child placed in a more appropriate group of children who are more willing to accept your child as she or he is.

Most important of all, I would have been frequently reminded that I was unique and talented instead of only being told, at school, that I was lazy, willful, and not living up to my potential—and being told, at home, that I was a disappointment and embarrassment to the family. I'm sure that my parents really did love me, but in their frustration and disappointment, they forgot to tell me about their love. I wouldn't be surprised to learn that my teachers were impressed with some of my special skills, but I never heard their praise, only their lectures about my shortcomings.

As a child with AS, I needed acceptance and affirmation most of all. I needed to work from a base of high self-esteem about all the good in me, not struggle to dig myself out of a pit of despair caused by focusing only on all my failings.

Every child with AS needs to know she or he is loved and accepted for who she or he is. Now, as an adult, I'm able to love and accept myself. But, the struggle to come to this place of self-esteem would not have been so monumental if a positive self-image had been nurtured in me from an early age. I can't stress how vital it is to help children with AS believe in themselves and their inherent goodness and worth.

≈

LESLEY JONES *was born into a middle-class, suburban family in 1967, years before teachers and therapists knew how to recognize Asperger's syndrome (AS). Instead, she was first labeled mentally retarded and then willfully disobedient and emotionally disturbed. Due to lack of proper interventions, she had to carve her own life out of a frustrating muddle of unexplained difficulties and lack of understanding. Growing up never took away the AS but eventually made it easier to live with.*

Lesley has been a high school dropout, homeless, and a mental patient. She has worked in horse stables and kitchens and traveled throughout the United States. She is currently a college student, studying mathematics. She finds joy in writing, reading, playing music, solving puzzles, spirituality, and science. She has found a life partner (also an eccentric), has nurtured pets, found friends and community online, and has managed to create the happy, fulfilled life that she was never expected to have.

GROUPS OFFER VALUABLE LIFE LESSONS

Nancy Witt

WHEN PARENTS FIRST LEARN that their child has a disability, they are overwhelmed with a cacophony of well-intended, but often contradictory, advice from doctors, therapists, psychologists, teachers, friends, and family members. While grieving for the loss of those fantastic dreams they had when the child was in utero and building new dreams that acknowledge their new reality, parents sift through this advice—accept it, reject it, challenge it, or modify it, to meet the needs of their family.

Building new hopes and dreams takes time. But, at some point, parents, usually with the assistance of some professionals, begin planning for the future as they recognize their child's individuality, gifts, and potential. Collaborating with physicians, therapists, educators, and psychologists, parents work to optimize learning opportunities, to maximize the child's independence, and to minimize health care concerns. Over time, parents learn to advocate for their children. And, as the children themselves develop, they learn how to advocate for themselves, often from adults with disabilities.

Unfortunately, few young people with disabilities learn how to be a part of a group. In contrast, from an early age, children without disabilities learn how to participate in all sorts of groups. They go out for soccer, Little League, and basketball. They join Daisies, Cub Scouts, 4-H, Campfire, Boys and Girls Clubs, community arts programs, and religious youth fellowship groups. Yet, even though many of these groups have taken steps to be more accommodating to potential members with disabilities, few children with disabilities join such groups. This is very troubling because all children need to learn how to interact, make friends, and work with people different from themselves.

Joining a team or a group will help to improve a child's interpersonal skills. Coaches, team captains, band directors, and debate team sponsors all convey important information verbally and nonverbally that enable groups of people to work together for a common goal. Learning how to listen and really hear what someone is saying improves a person's ability to receive and give directions. It also can lead to greater empathy among people with different life experiences.

Similarly, learning how to speak, whether it is in a one-on-one situation with a classmate, in a debate with an opponent, or before a large audience is also important. Speaking can teach respect for another person's perspective and experience, even if it is vastly different than your own.

Team sports, after-school programs and clubs, artistic and intellectual activities, and ordinary hangouts provide children with opportunities to develop friendships and their own networks of support. But being a child with a disability can be a very isolating experience because, in part, they happen to live in a world that is more suited for young people without disabilities.

Group activities can teach responsibility and follow-through. Young people often struggle with taking responsibility for their actions and inactions, and young people with disabilities can sometimes try to use their disability as an excuse for their irresponsibility. In group activities, a young person also needs to learn how to maintain her or his cool and sense of humor, even when things aren't going the way she or he expected.

Children with disabilities need to develop friendships with people outside of their immediate families. Making friends will improve a child's interpersonal communication skills, social skills, patience, understanding of others, dependability, and, because true friends hold each other accountable for their actions and inactions, a sense of responsibility. Friendships can also help a child gain independence and a social network of people who are helpful and mutually supportive.

Since we live in a diverse world, I believe that at least half of these friendships should be outside of the disability community. Friendships with others with disabilities can provide emotional support and practical advice—but may be isolating and limiting. Friendships outside the disability community can help a child gain perspective and maturity. Community recreation programs and youth organizations are two types of groups that work to integrate children with disabilities with their nondisabled peers.

Today's workplace is filled with teams of people from different backgrounds who come together as a group every day, or for relatively short periods of time, to complete a project, meet a goal, or finish a task. In addition to the workplace, civic, recreational, professional, and religious organizations in every community bring people together in groups—to educate members, socialize, raise money for good causes, and so on.

In the current information age, more and more people with disabilities are well educated, intelligent, and working. And, people with disabilities will be needed to fill tomorrow's jobs—jobs that will rely more upon talent, persistence, and ingenuity than upon physical strength and flexibility.

Many employers are willing to purchase equipment, modify buildings, and change job responsibilities to accommodate someone's physical or cognitive disability. But, employers are rarely willing to retain employees who are habitually late, use their disability as an excuse to miss work, or don't finish tasks assigned to them. While still in school, a young person with a disability can learn basic job skills via volunteer work, job-shadowing experiences, internships, and part-time employment. Parents, educators, and the business community need to work together to create these opportunities.

Businesses and organizations that have people with disabilities as their clientele are striving to become more diverse and to reflect more accurately the people they serve. While this is a good thing, sometimes people with disabilities accept leadership positions that they haven't been adequately prepared for and cannot carry out. Unprepared leaders with disabilities then become tokens. No one can be a leader all of the time—being a part of a group at a young age can help a child learn when it is appropriate to be a leader and when it is appropriate to be a participant. Being part of a group can also gradually teach a child the leadership skills needed to help the group accomplish its goals. Leaders need to be able to delegate responsibilities, identify skills and strengths in others, help people reach consensus, hold people accountable for their decisions and nondecisions, and understand budgets and organizational goals.

Parents know that there are many life lessons that a child needs to learn while growing up. The nature of those lessons changes as the child ages, but learning how to play and work with others in groups is something that children of all ages need to learn.

⁓

NANCY WITT *has cerebral palsy and some vision problems caused by being born too soon. She is an associate with State Public Policy Group, an Iowa-based public affairs/association management firm, and its sister organization, SUMO Group, an administrative services firm. She provides organizational development, issue management, and policy development services to clients primarily in the areas of public affairs, health, human services, diversity, technology, and dis-*

ability. Nancy works closely with groups in constituency development activities and developing and implementing policy advocacy efforts. She provides government relations support and assists in writing weekly summaries of pending legislation. In addition, she leads and assists in meeting facilitation, research, and writing. She has a degree in communications/public relations from the University of Northern Iowa and now lives in Grundy County, Iowa, with her parents.

CREATING AN INDIVIDUAL

Lisa A. Bertolini

L AST SUMMER, I attended my first national conference for people with my disability, spinal muscular atrophy. Before arriving,
due to the typical prognosis for individuals with the disease, I
expected that the majority of individuals with disabilities present
would be children. At the meeting, when I saw the great number of
beautiful children flying around in their electric wheelchairs and the
number of young parents seeking answers, I suddenly found myself
feeling pity for these children that I never felt for myself. I have
already survived the physical and emotional obstacles that these children had yet to face.

As one of the few adults with the disease present, many parents
were quick to ask me questions during breaks. I found myself wanting to give them three pieces of advice that I wish all parents could
read in a handbook, advice that wasn't made available to my parents
so long ago. First, promote your child's sense of independence. Second, remember to take care of yourself as well as your child. And
third, prepare in the event that you are no longer there to be the caregiver for your child.

One of the greatest gifts that a parent can bestow on a child with
a disability is to help that child develop a sense of self. As easy as it
can be to take control and be the main source of your child's per-

sonal care, refrain from making all your child's decisions. Empower your child with the ability to develop his or her own personality, not yours.

I will always be grateful to my parents for allowing me to make one of the single most important decisions of my life. When I was twelve years old, my neurosurgeon suggested a spinal fusion. If the decision had remained with my parents, the answer would have been no—fear would have stopped them. From my perspective, I was reaching adolescence and wanted to look pretty and wear clothes just like my peers. I never regretted my decision to go forward with the surgery.

Teach your child to speak up for herself or himself. Don't answer questions that are addressed to your child. Above all, rather than thank others for assisting your child, teach your child to develop manners of her own.

When I was heading toward college, almost all the students with disabilities that I knew decided to major in computer science. My mother took for granted that was the natural career path I would choose as well. But my first love was accounting. Although this caused many an argument at home, I had to be allowed to make my own decision. It was the wrong one, but it was *my* wrong one!

I consider my room my personal space. My mother likes to keep my room neat and pretty for my personal enjoyment because she loves me. At times, though, I find items that I consider a treasure, or things that I know need to be within reach in the near future, relocated because my mother maintains tidiness. I try to emphasize that my room is what I pay rent for (and yes, as your child matures allow them to pay rent) and I want to express myself in it.

Interestingly, I find myself making similar mistakes when it comes to my mother and her battle with cancer. All too often, I speak on her behalf with her doctors. I even try to dictate how she should eat. Each day I have to remind myself that I cannot make lifestyle choices for her. I can only provide her with information and hope that she

makes the best life choices for herself. Just because she has a difficult disease, just as I do, she is not less of a person or less capable of
making her own choices.

In helping your child to make a life for himself, don't forget to
make a life for yourself. Today, children don't have the privilege that
I had of having my mother home all the time. Although I certainly
benefited from this arrangement, I fear that it didn't help my mother
to develop her own interests. Do not feel guilty for making time
for yourself! You and your child are a loving team. Not scheduling
time for themselves can make parents burned-out, depressed, and
resentful.

My mother's cancer faces us every day. On the rare opportunities that I have to get away, I have constant guilt for wanting the
break for myself. The wonderful part of this comes from actually
missing my mother and coming back to her refreshed—with a new
determination to go on.

Don't try to live through your child. Sometimes I fear that my
mother lost a sense of herself in trying to give me a wonderful life.
My mother saw me through college, through my career, and through
my relationships—but she had none of these for herself. When all is
said and done, I do not want to be the reason that she feels she
missed out on life.

Don't make your child's relationships your relationships. Each of
you needs time to share friends and to be alone with friends. Part of
making a life for yourself and promoting your child's independence
is to give her time alone with friends. It actually took my mother's
cancer—and her being less able to care for me—to finally enable her
to reestablish grammar school friendships and enjoy time with her
friends. Recently, she has been going for manicures. And, after fifty
years of marriage, my parents have finally begun taking trips without me.

Last, and most important, please do not hide from discussing
death. The possibility of your passing on before your child may be

beyond comprehension, but it is always a possibility. One of the greatest gifts that you can give your child is the ability to know that she can manage her own life. The only benefit from my mom's hospitalization is that I have developed confidence in myself. Now I know that I can take care of myself.

I can advertise for a personal care attendant (PCA). I can manage my own care. I can find people to clean my home. But I still need to improve my skills at firing people!

Unfortunately, no one will ever care for your child the way that you do. Each PCA will do the job in a different manner. Your child has to be able to ask for help in a way that works for him. When life was good and my mother was healthy, I almost never felt disabled—despite being disabled since birth. My mom is like an extension of me. With her around, I never have to ask for anything. The first time I hired a PCA, I could not believe how many favors I had to ask for! I never realized how much work I am!

Besides being able to manage physical care, it is imperative that your child be provided for financially. Wills and death are horrible topics to discuss. However, I cannot stress enough the importance of this topic. My parents avoided the topic—my mother promised me she would live to be one hundred years old. Parents need to find financial and legal advisors knowledgeable about the laws that pertain to the individuals with disabilities—and especially, the benefits of a Special Needs Trust. Ensure that your child will always have a home and someone to watch over her. No matter how difficult this topic is to face, parents and children will be relieved when it is done.

With respect, I hope that parents will consider my suggestions for a family growing together. When each family member is able to grow as a separate individual, with separate interests and relationships, they can come together to be an effective team.

～

BORN WITH *spinal muscular atrophy, Lisa Bertolini has always needed a wheelchair. She is the youngest of five children and the only one with spinal muscular atrophy. Mainstreamed into "regular" classes beginning in kindergarten, she graduated cum laude from Northeastern Illinois University. Even with pneumonia as a frequent companion, she has maintained steady employment since age sixteen, in large part because of her mother's dedication to making it possible. Although she worked many years away from home, as she gets older, it becomes more difficult. She presently works for Accenture full-time from home, serving as a data center relationship manager.*

Every day, Lisa thanks God for her caring family, for whatever strength she has that day, and for the assistance of the Muscular Dystrophy Association and Families of Spinal Muscular Atrophy.

AFTERWORD: DISABILITY CULTURE

John D. Kemp

BORN WITH ARMS ENDING just above the elbows and legs ending near the knees, I didn't know I was different until about age three, maybe four, when a young boy, very angry at me, said something hurtful. I went immediately to my dad for comfort and protection. For the first of many times, he told me that I was different—not better, worse, or special—than other children and that other children who couldn't accept me for using prostheses had problems, not me.

Thank you, Dad, for giving me the gift of pride in being equal as well as different. My dad is my hero for his life of devotion to family and faith, public service and advocacy, and personal values and beliefs.

Our natural mother passed away three months after my younger sister, Mary, was born, leaving Dad to raise three children. Kathy, my older sister, was then five, and I was fifteen months old. At age thirty-two, my dad restarted his life—with three young children, two master's degrees, a deep Catholic faith, and without his partner. He committed then to a life of quality parenting and love, public service and advocacy, and improving the lives of people with disabilities. By the time he decided not to seek reelection to the City Council of Prairie Village, Kansas, in 2001, in his eighty-third year of life, he had completed sixty consecutive years of public service—from a county public roads worker to Kansas's Secretary of Transportation for eight years in the 1980s.

He spoke to us often about his career, stressing the importance of service to our fellow citizens. In addition to civilian and military service with the U.S. Navy in World War II, Dad was a volunteer leader with Easter Seals, long before, during, and after I had been chosen to serve as its 1960 Poster Child.

Dad felt it was an honor to serve others. From his days growing up on the homestead land of his parents in northeastern Montana, he always believed it was a privilege to live in America, that freedom needed protection, and that volunteerism required nurturing. He expected all his children to volunteer at community-based organizations, and we did—Scouts, Easter Seals, candy-striping at the hospital, and serving Mass at our Catholic Church. Dad practiced as he preached—providing a wonderful role model for me.

Dad used his wisdom, charm, and good fortune to find and marry Joan, our stepmother—our mother—in 1970. Dad now has Parkinson's disease, and he addresses its challenges with all the skills he has acquired—managing it and never letting it defeat him.

I was given the gift of love and self-worth by my family—Dad and my two incredible sisters. Inclusive school settings from kindergarten through Washburn University Law School also contributed to my self-worth. Dad's successful argument was not how much inclusion would benefit me; rather, it was how—as a result of my participation as the only child with a disability—all children in the school would learn that there are children with disabilities who belong in our communities, with their families, and in local schools.

My disability has given me both insight and perspective on human behavior. A simple social "handshake" with me because I wear prostheses (hooks for hands) has sent ordinary people into states of total confusion. I know I must guide people at these times.

As I travel by air frequently, giving speeches and serving my law clients, I find myself answering strangers' inquiries about what happened to me. The answers lie in my identity as a person with a disability and as a member of the disability culture. I am proud to be a person with a disability. While my experience as a person with a disability does not completely define me, it is an important part of who I am today.

People with disabilities have a culture of their own—just as African Americans, Hispanic Americans, women, and so on do. The notion that a culture of disability exists is anathema to some people; yet, it is fully understood by most adults who have lived with their disabilities for years. Typically, cultural phenomena are transmitted down through families, as lore and legend, and at places of worship. Our disability culture is transmitted from one of us to another, peer to peer. Yet, parents and families can nurture it. When my dad gave me my pride in being a person with a disability, he was nurturing a culture of disability within me. I urge parents and families to nurture our culture.

Carol Gill, Ph.D., an assistant professor in the Department of Disability and Human Development, College of Applied Health Sciences at the University of Illinois at Chicago, has articulated the core characteristics of our disability culture as follows:

- People with disabilities have a heightened acceptance of human differences—whether social, racial, economic, or class.
- People with disabilities consider interdependence an essential aspect of our lives.
- People with disabilities use humor—the ability to find something absurdly hilarious in almost anything, however dire—without it becoming self-deprecatory.
- People with disabilities have an ability, acquired over time living with our disabilities, to read others' attitudes and conflicts in order to sort out, fill in the gaps, and grasp the latent meaning in contradictory social messages.

We are connected as a culture because of shared indignities inflicted upon us by poor architectural planning and design and by others' stereotypically negative assumptions about us. We are also connected by the frustration and anger that wells up once in a while when we tire of dealing with prostheses, scooters, and sores—and that makes us search for understanding by someone who has been where we find ourselves. Anger, frustration, and hurt are managed quite well by many of us . . . and poorly by all of us once in a while. But how do we handle these emotions?

In his book *Emotional Intelligence: Why It Can Matter More Than IQ* (Bantam Books, 1995), Daniel Goleman, Ph.D., describes a core of emotional competencies: controlling impulses, managing anger, and finding creative solutions to social predicaments. Goleman estimates that only 20 percent of life's success is attributable to IQ points. The other 80 percent is emotional intelligence—the ability to rein in impulse, to read another's innermost feelings, and to handle relationships smoothly. I know I had the hardest time managing my own anger and frustration until I read something by Aristotle. Aristotle suggested that it is a rare skill to be angry in all the right ways (at the right person, to the right degree, at the right time, with the right purpose). I have been working on this skill, and I suggest that parents and children with disabilities consider it as they deal with the frustrations and anger that are part of our cultural experience. It is OK to be angry for a while. Then address the cause(s) of frustration and anger and fix it—or accept that you cannot change it.

I empathize with parents. From the beginning of pregnancy, you've prayed for and dreamed of "a healthy, happy, normal" baby. Your world flips over when your baby does not meet this standard. You might think, quite wrongly, it must be something you did or some genetic factor. Please be assured that it is not your fault. My dad and mom had similar concerns.

After Mom died, my dad's three sisters and his mother came to help. Dad left each of us with a sister for three months—to examine how his life had changed, why this tragedy would befall us, and what he could do going forward. None of us has ever known where he went, what he did, with whom he spoke, or what progress he made. When he returned, he gathered us up and we began as a family of four. He never looked back, other than to honor our mom and tell us what a kind, loving, and beautiful woman she was. Dad has never blamed her—or himself—for my disability.

Please don't blame yourselves. Come into this new world of people with disabilities with curiosity, criticism, and your own set of values for parenting your child. Find a new friend who is going through or has just completed such a journey, and then, with your friend's guidance and suggestions, enjoy parenting.

I believe that inclusion works, even for most children with severe disabilities. Sometimes, however, caring parents decide that more intensive services and supports in a separate, segregated setting are necessary. Such parents need not apologize. My philosophy is that "choice," the fundamental value of the disability civil rights movement, affords parents a full spectrum of options—including separate services. Families and children have the right to make that choice—a choice that must be respected by all.

Take care of your marriage. Raising a child with a disability or serious health concern can add stresses to any marriage. If divorce should become the solution, and I hope it does not, financial stresses will increase and all children must be protected from the pains that follow. Each child must always feel special and not a burden. Be sure to tell your children that your divorce is yours—they are not responsible for such parental decision making.

Finally, get a life! Keep the laughter and joy flowing and set and celebrate goals achieved as victories of life. For almost all children with disabilities, there will come a time when parents have to let go. So, teach them early the way to become independent and maintain that independence as well as their pride in themselves—pride in the differences and similarities of all people—and you will have done a terrific job as parents.

~

JOHN KEMP *is a principal in the law firm of Powers, Pyles, Sutter, &*
Verville, P.C., and has a federal disability law and legislative practice.
He is married and lives in downtown Washington, D.C.

A graduate of Georgetown University (1971) and Washburn Uni-
versity School of Law (1974), John was awarded an Honorary Doc-
torate of Law from Washburn in May 2003.

John has served as chief executive officer of United Cerebral Palsy
Associations and VSA Arts. Currently, he is the chief executive offi-
cer of the HalfthePlanet Foundation, Disability Service Providers of
America, and The Abilities Fund. He also serves as a member of sev-
eral nonprofit boards of directors, including the American Associa-
tion of People with Disabilities (cofounder) and the U.S. International
Council on Disabilities (chairman).

A much sought-after keynote speaker and humorist, John delivers
many major addresses each year before conferences, conventions, and
annual meetings.

RESOURCES FOR PARENTS AND FAMILY MEMBERS

WHEN PARENTS FIND OUT that a baby or young child has a disability or special health care need, they can

- Connect with experienced, nearby parents
- Seek early intervention services
- Get information about a child's special needs

Information on key Internet sites that can assist parents with each of these steps follows.

Connect with Experienced Parents

Parent Training and Information Centers (PTIs) in each state in the United States (and in U.S. territories) can connect parents with other parents and with other local resources. PTIs also provide training and information for parents of infants, toddlers, school-aged children, and young adults with disabilities as well as the professionals who work with their families. This assistance helps parents participate more effectively with professionals in meeting the educational needs of children and youth with disabilities. PTI staff members are experienced parents.

To find the PTI that serves each state or territory, go to taalliance .org/PTIs.htm and indicate the specific state.

The **National Information Center for Children and Youth with Disabilities** is a national information and referral center that provides information on disabilities and disability-related issues for families, educators, and other professionals. Its special focus is children and youth (birth to age twenty-two).

To identify services in your state, click on State Resources at nichcy.org/states.htm.

Seek Early Intervention Services

Early intervention programs are available in every state and territory in the United States. Research has demonstrated that early intervention is helpful for young children and their parents. The law establishing early intervention programs resulted in programs for babies and children (ages newborn to two; called Part C programs) and programs for preschool children (ages three to five; called Section 619). The terms *Part C* and *Section 619* refer to specific sections of the legislation that established these programs.

To find the person responsible for early intervention programs (including telephone numbers and e-mail addresses) for babies and children (ages newborn to two) in every state and territory, go to nectac.org/contact/ptccoord.asp.

To find the person responsible for early intervention programs (including telephone numbers and e-mail addresses) for preschool children (ages three to five) in every state and territory, go to nectac .org/contact/619coord.asp.

Get Information

National disability specific organizations provide a great deal of useful information, including how to contact local chapters. When a child's specific diagnosis is uncertain, parents can ask professionals to identify conditions that a child may have so that parents can review available information.

The **National Information Center for Children and Youth with Disabilities** site, referenced previously, includes a vast list of national disability organizations at nichcy.org/pubs/genresc/gr2.htm, including clearinghouses of information on specific disabilities or conditions.

When a child has a relatively rare condition, parents can get information at the website of the **National Organization of Rare Disorders** at rarediseases.org.

The **Fathers Network** (fathersnetwork.org) provides wonderful information especially for dads. The mission of the Fathers Network is to celebrate and support fathers and families raising children with special health care needs and developmental disabilities. Mothers are welcome.

Families are concerned about their "other" children—children without disabilities. The **Sibling Support Project** is a fine resource at thearc.org/siblingsupport.

DisabilityResources.org (disabilityresources.org) is a virtual library of information about websites serving the disability community. Disability Resources combs the Web regularly to find the best resources available, reviews each site, and then organizes them by topic or disability. This is a wonderful site because it provides helpful reviews of the sites, not merely links.

The **DRM WebWatcher** (disabilityresources.org/DRMwww.html) is an easy-to-use online subject guide to the best disability resources on the Internet. It features hundreds of topics and disabilities, each on a separate page. Each topic or disability page includes links to the best websites, documents, databases, and other informational materials of national or international interest.

The **DRM Regional Resource Directory** (disabilityresources .org/DRMreg.html) is a guide to state and local agencies and organizations in the United States, organized by state.

The **Family Village** (familyvillage.wisc.edu/index.htmlx) is a global community of disability-related resources. It integrates information, resources, and communication opportunities on the Internet for persons with cognitive and other disabilities, for their families, and for those who provide services and support. It includes informational resources on specific diagnoses, communication connections, adaptive products and technology, adaptive recreational activities, education, worship, health issues, disability-related media and literature, and more.

The **Religion and Disability Program** (nod.org/religion) of the National Organization on Disability (N.O.D.) is an interfaith effort, urging national faith groups, local congregations, and seminaries to identify and remove barriers of architecture, communications, and attitudes. It provides interfaith guides to assist congregations to become more welcoming to people with disabilities of all ages and their families.

The **STARBRIGHT Foundation** (starbright.org) helps to empower seriously ill children to live richer, more fulfilling lives. Using an innovative combination of technology, health care, and entertainment, STARBRIGHT strives to ensure that no child need sacrifice quality of life to an illness. Its programs are creative blends of medical information and emotional support designed to fill critical gaps in health information, offer seriously and chronically ill children a sense of peer support, validate their feelings, and help them to develop crucial coping skills.

The **CanChild Centre for Childhood Disability Research** (fhs .mcmaster.ca/canchild) is a center (located in Hamilton, Ontario, Canada) for childhood disability research that seeks to maximize the quality of life of children and youth with disabilities and their families. Research programs at CanChild concentrate on children and youth with disabilities and their families within the context of the communities in which they live. Its focus is on the interrelationships between individuals, their families, communities, and health systems.

The **HalfthePlanet Foundation** (halftheplanet.org) was created to be the authoritative online source of reliable tools for independent living for the disability community. It is dedicated to the belief that only when the barriers to accessibility are removed and practical solutions to everyday life are provided can all people live independent and fulfilling lives. The Internet site provides information and resources.

DisABILITIESBOOKS.com (DisABILITIESBOOKS.com) offers books, videos, and other products of interest to parents, children and adults with disabilities, and professionals.